CRICUT DESIGN SPACE &

PROJECT IDEAS MASTERY:

2 Books in 1

Beginner'S Guide To Master A Cutting
Machine (Maker, Explore Air, Joy). Coach
Playbook With Tips And Illustrations To
Explore To Become Expert

Lorrie Paper - Jennifer Cutter

TABLE OF CONTENTS

CRICUT DESIGN SPACE FOR BEGINNERS

TABLE OF CONTENTS

CRICUT PROJECT IDEAS FOR BEGINNERS

CRICUT DESIGN SPACE FOR BEGINNERS:

A Diy Book That Will Guide You Step-By-Step To Design Project Ideas With The Cutting Machines. A Coach Playbook With Tips And Illustrations

Introduction

The Cricut design studio program enables you to view before you cut, which is a substantial newspaper saver.so you break down and purchase the Cricut design studio program. You start it up and determine there is a program disc, user guide about the very best way to set up the program, and a few necessary conditions and applications, a USB cable, and a cunning mouse pad that is configured. You load the app onto your computer, and following that, if you are like me, you mentioned: "what the hell do I do?"

Here are just a few items that have helped me with all of the Cricut design studio software, and it will help you.

1. Loaded within this Cricut design studio software package is the accessibility to all or any cartridges. Another fantastic element of this application is that with every new round that is readily available that you purchase, you might get on the internet and update your software to the latest edition. Considering the Cricut design studio app has all the current capsules, you are going to be able to record those that you do not need and then purchase or put on you want list. Notice: you are going to be able to utilize each cartridge that is about the Cricut design studio software, however you need to find that cartridge packaged in your Cricut cutter to lessen the image.

2. The manual describes welding. Welding is connecting letters or graphics. The welding feature is excellent if analyzing phrases or words. It will produce the tradition of sticking to your scrapbook page or greeting card super easy. When trimming letters that are not welded together, you need to be cautious they are implemented directly as well as the spacing is best.

3. Even the Cricut design studio app has a feature that lets you use quite a few capsules whenever you are creating a layout. This is not any matter with this particular Cricut design studio program. The moment your Cricut is cutting, it is likely to allow you to understand just what cartridge to load in your Cricut cutter. How cool is that? Even the Cricut design studio program will enable you to create anything that your imagination will allow. There are unlimited possibilities of your creativeness employing the Cricut design studio program.

Many crafting lovers have fallen in love with their email system, " the Cricut. A brand-new addition to this popular product is that the growth of a software program created just for Cricut users.

The Cricut design studio is a computer program application produced by Provo craft, the artists of the Cricut machine. Although the system itself empowers the user to cut unique fonts and shapes in a range of measurements, the Cricut design studio takes it into an entirely new level. Connect the circuit to the computer with a USB port, install the program, and unleash a new measurement of crafting.

The principal benefit of the Cricut design studio is your capacity for customers to weld, or perhaps link letters together with one another to form a single cutting edge. Gone are the instances of copying each letter at one time. Now letters, phrases, words, and shapes can be plotted together before cutting, making it faster and simpler than ever to add cuttings to jobs.

Chapter 1

Getting to Know Design Space

C ricut machines, at the core, are really cool printers. Technically, they die cutters and creative planners that help you put together cool designs for various items that you want to make. There are a lot of models out there, and many great types to choose from.

The Explore series of machines contain software called Cricut Design Space, which allows for you to design in the space whatever you want to make, and then literally print it out.

If you are sick and tired of making the same images each time, or you are looking to cut out a design in vinyl without tearing your hair out, then a Cricut machine could really help you.

Models Overview

There are four main types of Cricut machines, all of which are used to cut out various designs. There are also the Legacy machines, such as the Cricut Expression, the Cricut Expression 2, and the Cricut Explore. You can also find the Cricut Cuttlebug, but this is a machine that is primarily used for embossing and die-cutting, and as of spring 2019, this item is discontinued.

Cricut Maker

So, you have the Cricut maker – the newest cutting machine – and it has a lot of new features. You can cut unbonded fabric with this, so you will not need to buy a stabilizer or a tiny rotary blade. It can also cut thicker materials, even balsa wood or thicker leather, and it can score items with a scoring wheel. This system is used with a variety of tools, which we will get into. It is the priciest option at $399, but for that price, you will be able to do a whole lot with it.

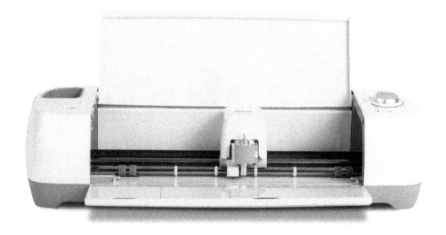

Cricut Explore One

The second model we will tackle here is the cheapest one, which is the Explore One. It is pretty basic, but for under $200, you are getting a great machine to start with. Personally, this is my favorite for beginners, since you can cut precisely, score, write, and do a lot more with it, and you do not need to use cartridges. It is not Bluetooth-enabled like the other devices, so you need to run a cord from the device you are using to create the design to the Cricut machine. Again, this is not really a problem, especially if you are someone who uses your engine a lot. This also is not wireless, but if you will not be using your computer or iPad in another room, this is not an issue.

It is not a double tool cartridge, either, so you will not be able to score and cut at the same time, but it can be done separately. However, this is not a problem unless you have to do both.

Cricut Explore Air

Then, there is the Cricut Explore Air, which is literally one step up from the first model. It has Bluetooth compatibility, and also has a second tool holder, basically doing what the first model could not. It is a helpful upgrade, and for only $50 more, you really cannot complain.

Cricut Explore Air 2

Your next step up is the Cricut Explore Air 2, which again, is another $50 increase from the previous model discussed. This one is another small model, and it is super-fast – faster than the Air 1. This is great for most of the materials that you want to cut, and the best part is that it does not take long to get the job done.

The primary difference with this one is that it is also pretty to look at, as well. If you like pastel colors, this might be one to consider – but again, the price could be a little hefty for those just starting out with Cricut machines.

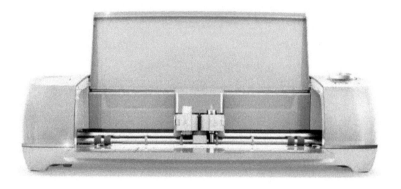

Tools

Cricut machines can also be used with a ton of tools, and most of them are pretty straightforward to use. Here are some of the best tools to consider for your machine:

· Wavy tool: Helps you cut waves into your design.

·   Perforation tool: Helps to make perforated markings in your design.

·   Weeding tool: This is one of the best tools to use when working with vinyl because it helps with peeling vinyl from the backing sheets.

·   Scraping tool: This helps remove any tiny pieces off of the design and prevents the material from moving around.

·   Spatula: This is a great one because it helps with moving the design off the backing without tearing material and can keep it free of debris.

·   Tweezers: These are good for pulling the tiny pieces of vinyl or other design elements from the middle without pulling the edges or tearing them.

·   Scissors: Cricut scissors are durable, made of stainless steel with micro-tip blades – perfect for detailed work.

·   Paper trimmer: This is really convenient with straight cuts, so you do not need to use scissors or a ruler. It is essential for working with vinyl.

·   Brayer: If you are using fabric or larger pieces of vinyl, this is actually one of the best tools to keep the material stabilized on your mat so the mat itself is not damaged.

·   Backup mats: This should be obvious, but if you are going to work with larger projects, the carpets do lose their stickiness after a while. This can prevent you from having to leave your project to pick up more.

·   Easypress Tool: This is awesome for iron-on vinyl that you do not want to iron. It also holds the vinyl much better, even if you wear it a lot, and eliminates the temperature and time guesswork you may otherwise have to do. It is a little pricey, but there are beginner options.

·   Brightpad: Finally, you have a Brightpad, which helps make the lines that you need to cut more visible. If you are doing more than just one cut, this is handy, since it will help with tracing, and with adapting the patterns, too.

These tools are essential, and to pick up the first few on the list, you will want to get the toolset, since it is much cheaper. But if you are going to be using your machine a lot, I highly recommend spending a little extra by picking up tools to use with it.

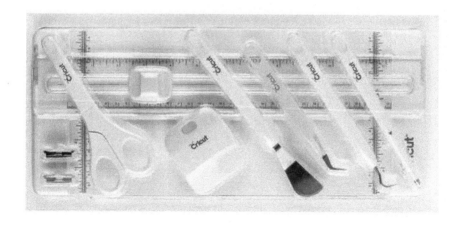

Accessories

The accessories and tools often do overlap in some ways, since a lot of these tools are accessories, such as the perforation tool and scraping tools. However, there is more available than just that, and below, you will learn of the essential accessories that can help you make the most of your machine.

· Deep cut blade: This helps you cut wood and leather, and you can buy these individually.

· Bonded fabric blade: This can cut through fabric that has been bonded with stabilizers such as Heat N Bond.

· Cutting Mats: These will be used for crafting pretty much anything, and if you are using lighter materials or more massive lines, you should get both a LightGrip and a secure grip cutting mat. These are useful for a variety of projects.

· Toolsets: they are essential to help you with your Cricut projects.

· Scoring Stylus: While the Maker model has this included, picking up scoring stylus accessories for other models can help you make anything requiring precise folding. These can help you fold pretty much any project by giving you neat score lines, taking out all the guesswork!

· Pens: These are useful for not just for scoring and cutting, but also writing –you can address letters and cards directly from your Cricut machine. No more signing a bunch of tags!

·   Aluminum Foil Ball: Hey, look – a Cricut accessory that is not something you need to go to a craft store or Amazon for! This will keep your blades clean and sharp, so you do not need to spend extra money buying replacements. Plus, you do not have to travel far to find it, you may even have some in your kitchen!

·   Fabric Marking Pen: If you plan on using your Cricut machine for cutting fabric, this is something that you should consider buying. It will save you a bunch of time.

These accessories are items that you either already have or items that you may not have even thought about. But purchasing a few of these will certainly help you use your Cricut machine, that is for sure.

Cricut Access

Cricut Access is the software that gives you access to images, fonts, and the like. You will need to purchase this if you plan on using your Cricut machine, period, and if you do not have the software already, I suggest buying it.

The monthly option is perfect for beginners and offers over 400 different fonts and 90,000 different images. And it comes with a 10% savings on any additional Cricut purchases you need, as well as a 10% savings on premium images and fonts, such as Disney fonts. You will also have access to a priority member line.

The next membership option is annual, which is precisely the same as the basic, but you do not have to pay as much – just $7.99 per month, upfront. It is useful if you are serious about getting into Cricut.

Finally, you have the premium option, which is the same price as monthly and offers unlimited access to the same fonts and images, savings on both products and licenses, and a 50% extra savings on licensed pictures and fonts, along with some ready-to-make projects. If you spend over $50 on the Cricut store, you earn free shipping. Personally, I think this is the best option if you plan on spending a lot of money on Cricut items, and you are in it for the long haul. However, if you are just beginning, the monthly membership is probably a better choice, because you can cancel this at any time.

Membership allows you to save a little bit on premium ideas and licensed designs – the more you make with your Cricut machine, the more you save, and you'll realize that you could save a lot really fast. On average, customers say that they make up the subscription costs with the money they collect, and the coolest thing is that there is so much to choose from, you can find some beautiful designs. It is definitely great if you want exclusive content.

Cartridges

The final item you will need is, of course, Cricut cartridges. These are little cartridges that you put into the machines that are loaded with different fonts, images, and graphics. You can buy themed cartridges, too, with the idea to create the design that the Cricut machine will make for you.

There are many different ways to use just one cartridge, even though the designs are limited.

Now, if you are getting the Cricut access package, this might not be worth it, but for those of us who don't want to pay for a subscription service yet and just want to cut things, this could be an excellent option to try out.

You can also import images, of course, with the Cricut design space on the most current machines, and these machines also work with Cricut cartridges. For crafters who do not want to design their cuts, this is ideal. You can also use both together, and there are benefits to this, too.

To use the cartridge, you just put it into the machine, go to Design Space, and then follow the steps. Once they are linked up, you can necessarily choose the cartridge you want to work on, and you are ready to go. The advantage of this system is that there are a lot of rounds you can get, each with unique designs, and once they are linked up, you can mix and match them quite easily.

Chapter 2

Project Design

Cricut Project Ideas to Try!

With Cricut, the ideas for projects are so vast, you will be amazed at how much you can do. So, what are some ideas that could work for you? Here are a few that you can consider, and some of the best project ideas for those who are stumped on where to begin!

Easy Projects

Custom Shirts

Custom shirts are incredibly comfortable. The beauty of this is, you can use the Cricut fonts or system options, and from there, you can simply print it on. Personally, I like to use the iron-on vinyl because it is easy to work with. Just take your image and upload it into Design Space. Then, go to the canvas and find the image you want. Once you have selected the image, you click on the whitespace that will be cut – remember to get the insides, too. Make sure that you choose reduced image, not print from cut image, and then place it on the canvas to the size of your liking. Put the iron-on vinyl shiny side down, turn it on, and then select iron-on from the menu. Choose to cut, and make sure you mirror the image. Once done, pull off the extra vinyl to remove the plastic between the letters. There you go! A simple shirt.

Vinyl Decals

Vinyl can also be used to make personalized items, such as water bottle decals. First, design the text – you can pretty much use whatever you want for this. From here, create a second box and make an initial, or whatever design you want. Make sure that you resize this to fit the water bottle, as well.

From here, load your vinyl, and make sure that you use transfer tape on the vinyl itself once you cut it out. Finally, when you adhere the lettering to the bottle, go from the center and then push outwards, smoothing as you go. It takes a bit, but there you have it – pure water bottles that children will love! This is a beautiful, simple project for those of us who are not really that artistically inclined but want to get used to making Cricut items.

Printable Stickers

This is super simple and fun for parents and kids. The Explore Air 2 machine works best.

With this one, you want the print then cut feature, since it makes it much more comfortable. To begin, go to Design Space and download images of ice cream or whatever you want, or upload pictures of your own. You click on a new project, and on the left side that says images, you can choose the ones you like, and insert more of these on there.

From here, choose the image and flatten it, since this will make it into one piece rather than just a separate file for each. Resize as needed to make sure that they fit where you are putting them.

You can copy/paste each element until you are done. Once ready, press saves, and then choose this as a print then cut image. Click the big button at the bottom that says make it. Make sure everything is right, then press continue, and from there, you can load the sticker paper into the machine. Make sure to adjust this to the right setting, which for sticker paper is the vinyl set. Put the paper into there and load them in, and when ready, the press goes – it will then cut the stickers as needed.

From there, take them out and decorate. You can use ice cream or whatever sticker image you want!

Personalized Pillows

Personalized pillows are another fun idea and are incredibly easy to make. To begin, you open up Design Space and choose a new project. From here, select the icon at the bottom of the screen itself, choosing your font. Type the words you want, and drag the text as needed to make it bigger.

You can also upload images, too, if you want to create a large picture on the pillow itself.

From here, you want to press the attach button for each box, so that they work together, and both are figured when centered, as well.

You then press make it – and you want to turn to mirror on, since this will, again, be on iron-on vinyl. From here, you load the iron-on vinyl with the shiny side down, the press continues, follow the prompts, and make sure it is not jammed in, either.

Let the machine work its magic with cutting and from there, you can press the weeding tool to get the middle areas out.

Set your temperature on the easy press for the right settings, and then push it onto the material, ironing it on and letting it sit for 10 to 15 seconds. Let it cool, and then take the transfer sheet off.

There you have it! A simple pillow that works wonders for your crafting needs.

Cards

Finally, cards are a great project idea for Cricut makers. They are simple, and you can do the entire project with cardstock.

To make this, you first want to open up Design Space, and from there, put your design in. If you like images of ice cream, then use that. If you want to make Christmas cards, you can do that, too. Basically, you can design whatever you want to on this.

Now, you will then want to add the text. You can choose the font that you want to use, and from there, write out the message on the card, such as "Merry Christmas." At this point, instead of choosing to cut, you want to select the right option – the make it option. You do not have to mirror this but check that your design fits appropriately on the cardstock itself. When choosing material for writing, make sure you select the cardstock.

From there, insert your cardstock into the machine, and then, when ready, you can press go and the Cricut machine will design your card.

This may take a minute, but once it is done, you will have an excellent card in place. It is super easy to use.

Cricut cards are a great personalized way to express yourself, creating a one-of-a-kind, sentimental piece for you to gift to friends and family.

Chapter 3

Using Images in Design Space

C ricut Design Space has thousands of images to choose from to enhance crafting projects. There is also the option to upload your own pictures into Design Space for use in your projects. This chapter takes a look at images, discusses how they are used in Design Space, and has an Exercise to follow to create a plan with images.

Images, Projects, and Templates

In Design Space you will come across images, templates, and projects.

Images are pictures that are loaded into the Cricut Image library or uploaded by the users. A copy can be a scanned drawing, an image created by a graphics program, drawn on a drawing tablet, a cartoon, a photo, and so on.

Projects may contain images, fonts, templates, and shapes. A project is a file containing a design being created to be cut-out on a cutting machine. You can create your own design projects from scratch. You can also customize a previously saved plan. Cricut comes with a library of hundreds of Ready-to-Make projects. These Cricut Ready-to-Make projects can be made as-is or customized to suit your design needs.

Templates are pre-drawn diagrams that can be customized to predefined settings. These images are not cut or printed; they are merely used as a placeholder on which to design a project. For instance, you may want to develop an iron-on logo for a tote bag. Cricut Templates options have a Tote bag template you can design around. Design Space has a model for just about every design.

Cartridges

Historically, Cricut cutting machines did not connect to a PC or Mobile device. They were stand-alone machines with small monitors and a keypad for writing text. If you wanted to add an image or font that was not a default font, you would have to purchase a cartridge.

Each cartridge came with a library of either fonts, images, or preset designs on them. There are over 350 different Cricut cartridges, each holding a library of pre-loaded pictures or fonts. This was very frustrating for users especially when only one map or font was required but you had to purchase the entire cartridge to get it.

The Cartridges were divided into Image groups, much like greeting cards. These groups were:

- Cards

- Events

- Everyday

- Holiday & Seasons

- Licensed Designs

- Cricut Imagine Library

o   Art

o   Colors & Patterns

o   Fonts

o   Patterns

Each one of these groups would have a number of image series such as Disney for Licensed Images, Toy Story for Licensed Images, Baseball for Everyday group, and Baby Shower for the Events group.

Cricut Image Library

Cricut soon started to transfer cartridges into digital download images and the Cricut Image Library was developed. This gave users a little more control over the images or fonts they purchased.

Cricut Design Space Image Library

The Cricut Design Space Image Library was developed from the cartridges and the original Cricut Image Library. It has hundreds of thousands of images that can be used in any project. With the Design Space Image library, a user has more control over which images they want to purchase. There is an option to have a Cricut Access membership which includes illustrations or to buy them individually as you design projects.

Cricut Design Space Access Image Library

Access membership gives users the advantage of having thousands of images that come with the privilege of membership. These are updated and added to each day. These are the Design Space images that have a green 'a' in the corner to let users know they belong to that library. All other photos will either have a price next to them or are for free.

Working with Images in Design Space

In this part, you are going to start a new project, Exercise. The Exercise will work with Images using some of the functions from Exercise 1 and 2 as well as a few more advanced features.

Exercise — Working with Images

This Exercise will teach you how to browse for images, manipulate them, and customize them. It will also cover how to purchase copies.

This Exercise Covers the Following Topics, Options, and Functions:

- Navigating the Images screen/Cricut Design Space Image Library

- Browsing and searching for images

- Browsing and searching for images with filters

- Selecting Images

- Purchasing images

- Working with the Color Sync Panel

- Using the Weld function

- Using Group/Ungroup

- Using the Flip function

- Introduction to the Flatten function

- Editing images with the Slice tool

- Editing images in Upload Mode

- Separating objects

Project Tools and Accessories:

- Active Design Space session

- PC with a Keyboard and Mouse

- Cricut cutting machine connected

Directions:

1. Open a new project in Design Space.

2. Select Images from the Design Panel on the left-hand side.

3. Things to take note of:

    1. The Main menu bar is still set to Canvas, the project name or untitled is still visible, as is My Project, Save, Cricut Machine, and the Make it button.

    2. The Design Panel is still accessible on the left-hand side of the screen.

3. The Edit menu directly below the Main menu bar has been replaced with the Images menu. This menu bar now contains:

1. Images — This option shows all the available models in the Cricut Design Space Library.

2. Categories — This option groups and filters all the images per Design Space predefined categories.

3. Cartridges — This option lists all the digital cartridges in the Design Space Library and will include any linked or already purchased cartridge. The Digital cartridges work much the same way as the physical Cricut Cartridges do. Each Cartridge will contain a whole lot of images on it.

4. Search Images Box — This box allows the user to search for an image based on a name, category, or image number.

5. Filter drop-down menu — The Filter drop-down menu will filter the image library displayed on the screen by the options selected in the drop-down

menu. These options include: Ownership Images, Type of Images, and Layered images.

6. Image Grid — This grid changes the number of images shown on the screen at one time.

4. The Canvas Workspace has changed to the Image Library.

5. At the bottom right-hand corner of the screen are two buttons: Cancel and Insert Images.

4. With the Images selected, in the Images menu bar scroll through the images to get an idea of the types of models available in the Design Space Image Library. Things to take note of while scrolling through the photos:

1. Does the image have a white 'a' in a green banner pinned to it?

2. Is the Image free or does it need to be paid for?

3. The Images are listed in alphabetical order.

4. Click on the 'i' in the circle at the bottom of the image on a few of the photos to see the extra information about the picture.

5. The information about the images will have the Image title, the Image Design Space number, and the creator of the Image listed on it. If the Image has a cost, there will be a "Buy Image" option.

6. Any writing in green on the Image information can be clicked on. This will bring up more images, if there are any, from that particular designer. Buy Image will take you to the shop to purchase the Image.

7. If, at any time, you want to get back to the main Image screen, click on Images on the Images menu bar.

5. With Categories on the Image menu bar selected browse through the different categories. Things to take note of:

1. Featured categories will have Free this Week where some of the images you may have to pay for are on special and can be used for free. Most popular will feature the Images that have been used the most recently. Lastly, the Recently Added category lists all the new Image additions to the Design Space Image Library.

2. The categories are grouped into groups such as Baby, Clothing and Accessories, and so on. Under each of these categories will be images only on that category. This makes it easier to search through hundreds of thousands of pictures looking for the one you need.

3. The Images menu bar reflects the name of the Category you are currently browsing.

4. To get back to the Main Categories listing, click on Categories on the Images menu bar.

6. With Cartridges on the Image menu bar selected, browse through the different categories. Things to take note of:

    1. The name of the Cartridge will be at the bottom left-hand corner of the cartridge.

    2. In brackets next to the Cartridge is the number of images that come with the cartridge when purchased.

    3. The price will be on the bottom right-hand corner of the Cartridge in green.

    4. Clicking anywhere on the Cartridge will open up the Cartridge listing all the images that come with it.

    5. You can buy each Image separately without having to buy the entire Cartridge.

    6. The first Image displayed in the Cartridge list is the Cartridge cover with the name of the Cartridge and the option to buy it.

    7. The Images menu bar reflects the name of the Cartridge you are currently browsing.

    8. To get back to the Main Cartridge listing, click on Cartridges on the Images menu bar.

7. You can use the Search box to search for an image while in Images or Cartridges mode. You will note that when you are in one of these modes the Search box text changes to:

    1. Images Mode — Search Images

2. Cartridges — Search Image Sets

3. Selected Cartridge — Search in "Selected Cartridge Set Name"

4. Select Category — Search in <Category Name>

While in one of the above modes, the Search Image Library will be restricted to that set of images.

You cannot search while in Category Mode, you have to choose a Category in order to use the Search bar.

8. Select Images on the Image menu bar.

9. Select the Filter drop-down menu. This menu will filter down the options above to show only images you have selected with the filters.

10. Select Ownership and click in the little box next to My Images. Notice that the Image Library has now changed to show the Free images and any Images you may have purchased. It will also show Images you have uploaded or Images that come with a Cricut Access membership account.

Chapter 4

Manage and Improve Your Cricut Machine

T he Cricut machine has been developed for a wide range of factors. Currently, most people may believe that this device is exclusively for creating scrap books, but it is not. The Cricut machine may be utilized for more things than creating scrapbooks.

In case you appear closes in a Cricut machine and you let your creativity go crazy, you can think of lots of great Cricut suggestions that will help you have a supply of existing or accessible give your personal satisfaction.

How you can clean your machine

As with any machine type, it is essential that you simply clean it to help keep it doing work in tip-top condition. This an excellent video which tells you exactly how to clean your machine:

Non-alcoholic Baby wipes are a fantastic choice for cleaning both the wipes and the machine

Double-check your settings

Always make sure you have your machine ready to cut the proper material type! You can do this by altering the knob on the device, or you can get it done by hand within the Cricut application.

In the Cricut Design Space program, it is going to give you adjustments for a lot of different cutting components far more than are on the knob on the device. It gets entirely with the material. I also love you can set the options in there; in the event the method is not cutting the substance precisely the strategy you need it to.

Keeping blades sharp

Blades will become dull after a while - and it is often a gradual transition. I remember when I eventually replaced the module of mine on the old machine of mine, and I did not realize how bad it had gotten.

I suggest having various blades for various types of substances which you cut regularly - thus one that is just for fabric, one for vinyl, etc. You can have another knife for elements that you do not utilize as frequently. Allow me to share the various blades which are available:

Serious Cut Blade (Cricut / Amazon)

Good Point Blade (Cricut / Amazon)

Rotary Blade (Cricut / Amazon)

Bonded Fabric Blade (Cricut / Amazon)

Blade (Cricut / Amazon)

You must cleanse the housing for the blade after every use. This could get gunky very merely. I have discovered that using compressed air is quite simple to work with.

Transfer paper is crucial for a lot of tasks - for use with vinyl. Nevertheless, you can use transfer paper a few times - therefore be sure you do not throw it out!

Be sure you cut the transfer newspaper down on the size you have to eliminate extra waste. When you do not wish to purchase the Cricut Transfer Paper, you can simply use regular of contact paper. It may help you save a couple of dollars!

Vinyl Tips and Where you can Find Vinyl

I believe when men or women think of cutting devices as Cricut, they think about vinyl. I know that is the first thing that will come to mind for me! Thus, I figure it is worth bringing up some suggestions for cutting with vinyl.

First, it is crucial to comprehend that there are lots of diverse types of vinyl - interior, gloss, matte, heat transfer, exterior, glittered…SO numerous. It is important to check out what type you are using to be able to cut it properly. For example, when I began utilizing heat transfer vinyl, it has taken me Forever to determine what side was meant to be cut

When you are getting prepared to cut the vinyl, ensure you line it up with the advantage of the mat and fills the whole mat. I usually have problems when I attempt to eliminate the actual place and size it in the actual right spot on the mat. Simply fill up the entire space!

After the vinyl is cut, I suggest cutting away extra vinyl before you eliminate it from the mat. When you do not do this, you chance to pull up vinyl which has not been cut.

If you perform the transfer to the transfer paper, it is simplest to accomplish this while it is still on the mat.

Start easy - vinyl comes with a learning curve, and yes it could be very easy to be frustrated with.

You can find vinyl a lot more of various places. I purchased an enormous package of vinyl from Amazon for cheap, even though it did the project, I did not feel as it had been the greatest quality. I simply like going with the Vinyl directly from the Cricut site or from Expressions Vinyl.

Be cautious with the fonts you make use of. I feel as if working with thicker fonts makes for a simpler time transferring and you do not risk breaking the style as a lot of. Basically, any font you purchase directly from Cricut is an excellent alternative.

Cricut Design Space

Cricut Design Space can be gotten to work with through their web-based program or by way of a mobile app. You have to have Internet access to make use of it, though it is where you will create all your designs.

You can come up with your own designs, or you can use designed templates. I love you can use the mobile app anyplace - it is very convenient when you are lying in bed or relaxing in the car.

Set Canvas in Cricut Design Space

This is one of the favorite features of mine of Design Space - it is a lot of guides for a wide variety of jobs. You simply choose the project, after which it overlays it in your design screen so you can ensure you get the sizing properly.

Cricut Access

If you are a major Cricut user and you wish to have access to their entire library of fonts and images, I believe this is well worth the investment. They have a number of plans which range from 4.99 to 9.99 dollars. You can learn which Cricut Access Plan is appropriate for you

You receive a chance to access more than 30,000 pictures, 370 fonts, many of project ideas, and you receive ten % off all of the purchases from Cricut.com.

Your own images and Fonts

You can make use of your own personal images and fonts within Cricut Design Space. In order to make use of your own font of yours, simply install a font which you have downloaded or purchased.

With pictures, on the left aspect of the Design Space platform, there is a function which states "Upload Images." You make use of this to publish the picture that you would like to cut - quite simple.

You can upload most, jpg,.svg,.gif,.png,.bmp, and then, Dxf documents & convert them into cuttable data. Etsy is loaded with lots of seriously great cut files which are great and inexpensive for just any occasions!

I suggest Fotor as a good spot to create your own designs. They have a free and paid account, & they are both excellent resources!

Cricut Mystery Box

This is one of my personal favorite things that Cricut does! Every month, they develop a "mystery box" of items - it is usually 29.99 to 39.99 dollars and it is loaded with resources and cartridges which are prized well past that. If you are somebody who simply loves creating and you are not looking for materials, this is a fantastic value. It will make for an excellent gift, too!

Do not forget to contemplate purchasing your Cricut Reference Printables! These are perfect and beautiful for every amount of Cricutter.

As that which was talked about before, people associate the usage of a Cricut machine with only making scrapbooks. Cricut device could be utilized to make fantastic calendars. The Cricut computer together with the Cricut Design Studio program could be utilized to think of designs for the calendar of yours.

One calendar year is composed of twelve months. Take note which every month includes a theme to it like being there, cold, and rainy could even be weeks which are notable for a certain occasion and the two tools that we simply mentioned, you can create and select designs that could breathe life into a certain month. Try letting make use of the month of December as a good example.

December is directly linked with Christmas and winter. Therefore in case, we had been creating a Cricut calendar depending on the month of December, you have to pick styles that might mirror the month. A number of fantastic models just for this month include reindeers, snowmen, and Santa clause himself. That is very cool would not you say.

Besides a Cricut calendar, the Cricut cutting device could be utilized to produce your own private gift cards. If you visit malls or to keep which specialize in selling gift cards, I am more or less positive you will remain to yearn for an alternative style.

With the usage of a Cricut machine coupled with the initiatives from the Cricut design studio, you can generate your gift card with the own design of yours and nobody will stop you. You are your own boss.

So these are several of the most popular Cricut ideas you can resort to that can help maximize the use of your Cricut machine. When you know of other ways apart from that which was simply tackled, you are free to apply it. It is a free world after all.

Chapter 5

Scrapbooking with Cricut Cartridges

You will find a thousand things which make the holiday season a headache. From accessories to presents, from budgets to children, from people to parents, it is that time of the year that you run out of ideas on what you need to gift your family, that time of year when you desire the very best decorative & most special components of your living room.

If you are confronted with that dilemma, buying a unique Cricut Cartridge may be your solution.

In case you are a novice to scrapbooking, you most likely have not heard of Cricut. And so first things first, what is a Cricut? Created by Provo Craft, Cricut is a house die cutting machine employed for cutting paper, cloth, and vinyl sheets into patterns.

And other things, the Cricut is frequently utilized for scrapbooking and paper crafting in which patterns like phrases, pictures, and styles are cut away to produce customized titles and accessories for pages. The device applies cartridges that have an assortment of themes, pictures, characters, and fonts to make cutouts of.

Having said that, below are reasons purchasing a holiday special Cricut Christmas Cartridge just could be the answer to your holiday headaches. If you present someone with a present, you want your gift to be different, unusual and something he/she does not currently have.

Scrapbooks fit that description quite effectively. And the new technology and gadgets developed each day, scrapbooking, liked as it had been, has become a dying trend.

You would barely see folks collecting items for their scrapbooks, not to mention gift for one another. Purchase a unique Cricut Christmas Cartridge, make an easy scrapbook or gift and page it to your best friend. That is a present he/she is going to keep for a long time.

Scrapbooks are private. And just who does not wish to present their loved ones with personalized gifts? Of course, everybody will love an Xbox or an iPhone, that is exactly why they create a huge number of stores selling electronic products.

But gifting your girlfriend a hand made a scrapbook with her amusing pictures individuals and eliminate in different shapes - which will simply be about probably the sweetest thing anyone is accomplished for her. Rest assured; she is yours forever.

And producing these kinds of a scrapbook does not demand a lot of your time in any event as you can constantly look for a Cricut Christmas Cartridge which contains heart shapes or other patterns you like.

The great thing about Cricut is the fact that you can find wide varieties of cartridges offered on the market to meet up with the demands of any event. Which means you wish to embellish your home with angel shaped cut-outs or pine shapes this Christmas, you will find Cricut Christmas cartridges readily

accessible. Or you are looking to host a themed Year that is a new party with special decorations of different patterns to match your theme, you will be amazed at the wide selection of Cricut cartridges you can get in the market.

The way you make use of your Cricut cartridges to help make this holiday season a unique one is just restricted by your own imagination. You could be as inventive as any & become a delight for your near and dear ones. From reindeer to an army of snowmen, from Christmas trees to villages, you can have all them with unique Cricut Christmas cartridges.

It is a breathtaking encounter I let you know! If you glance at the quality and supplies which the scrapbooks are produced of, you will feel the quantity of dedication and effort that the makers of these scrapbooks exerted simply to have the ability making them true.

That is precisely why individuals consider the art of making scrapbooks as a complex and delicate approach that will require a Lion's center and a load of dedication and patience. It is not a simple process as you have to conceptualize the design and after that create it.

You can only imagine what burden our ancestors must go through to be equipped to think of one scrapbook. However, in case you are taking a glance around you and analyze the way everything is continuing with using the scrapbook community, a lot more has changed.

Whenever you go into an exhibit of scrapbooks and you glance at the modern ones, you will find out how colorful the models of those are. You look at them and you begin to think about the way they had the ability to create those and above all the way they could create the style tangible. The answer is fairly easy.

When you would like to succeed in the art of scrapbooking, you want a Cricut cutting printer and a program. Just everyone owns a laptop, so I will not dig in a lot of into which. However, with the 2 aforementioned tools, these are prerequisites. The application device is the cause of the designs.

An important Cricut scrapbooking program is the Cricut Design Studio. Lots of scrapbook creators make use of this as it is a number of pre-loaded styles which could match some scrapbook maker's chosen theme! And so after the style have been selected, after this you instruct your laptop or computer to eliminate the style via your circuit cutting machine.

The Cricut cutting printer is practically responsible for cutting out the style you select out of your Cricut studio software. One Cricut cutting machine can set you back approximately 300 dollars and it is well worth every penny you spend so please do not have any 2nd thoughts of purchasing one.

In the event it comes to your scrapbooking, the right accessories can make all the difference. This is the reason it is a fantastic idea to decide Circuit accessories for your scrapbook needs to ensure you understand you are getting quality scrapbooking things you can rely on.

If you need help with your scrapbooking, Cricut is a title you can rely on to provide you with quality accessories and equipment to help you make a lot of scrapbooking. For instance, you can get your ideas and themes and cause them to become a reality of ways that you had not have been equipped to accomplish before.

Together with the Cricut slices and other accessories, you can be as creative as you would like. When you do not feel you are a rather inventive or artistic person, you can use these resources to make items you never ever would have been equipped to think of prior to. In case you are creative, you can take that create even more with the resources that Cricut can offer for you.

You can use these tools to your advantage to make several of the greatest scrapbooks around. The ideas of yours may rapidly turn into a reality so it is going to be easier than in the past to get all those pictures and mementos organized into scrapbooks so that you can treasure forever.

When selecting these accessories, make a summary of the people you want and require the best. Next, go down in order beginning with the people you will need the best and going right down to the people you would truly love to have as you can afford it. You can buy these one or two at a period before your collection is done and you have the great Cricut accessories you would like in your scrapbook collections.

Listed here are just some of the Cricut accessories available:

Serious Cut Blades

Cricut Stamp Refill

Cricut Jukebox

Cricut Cartridge Storage Box

Cricut Color Fashion

Cricut Cutting Mats

Cricut Spatula Tool

Selecting Cricut accessories for scrapbooking will make your scrapbooking easier that it provides you with more designs and more ways to use your creativity for superb scrapbooking. In order to add fun and color to your pages, know more concerning the usage of scrapbooking embellishments.

Chapter 6

Common List of Problems with Cricut Machine and How to Solve Them

Material Tearing or Not Cutting Completely Through

This is the biggest problem with most Cricut users. When this happens, the image is ruined, and you have wasted material. More machines have been returned or boxed up and put away due to this problem than any other.

But do not panic, if your paper is not cutting correctly there are several steps you can take to try and correct the problem.

Most important is this: Anytime you work with the blade TURN YOUR MACHINE OFF. I know it is easy to forget this because you are frustrated, and you are trying this and that to make it work correctly. But this is an important safety precaution that you should remember.

Make simple adjustments at first. Turn the pressure down one. Did it help? If not, turn the blade down one number. Also, make sure the mat is free of debris so the blade rides smoothly.

Usually the thicker the material, the higher the pressure number should be set to cut through the paper. Do not forget to use the multi cut function if you have that option. It may take a little longer to cut 2, 3 or 4 times, but by then it should cut clean through.

For those of you using the smaller bugs that do not have that option here is how to make your own multi-cut function. After the image has been cut, do not unload the mat just hit load paper, repeat last and cut. You can repeat this sequence 2, 3 or 4 times to ensure your image is completely cut out.

If you are using thinner paper and it is tearing, try reducing the pressure and slowing down the speed. When cutting intricate designs, you have to give the blade enough time to maneuver through the design. By slowing it down it will be able to make cleaner cuts.

Clean the edge of the blade to be sure no fuzz, glue or scraps of paper are stuck to it.

Make sure the blade is installed correctly. Take it out and put it back so it is seated firmly. The blade should be steady while it is making cuts. If it makes a shaky movement it is either not installed correctly, or there is a problem with the blade housing.

Be aware that there is a deep cutting blade for thicker material. You will want to switch to this blade when you are cutting heavy card stock. This will also save wear and tear on your regular blade. Cutting a lot of thick material will obviously wear your blade out quicker than thinner material and cause you to change it more often.

Machine Freezing

Remember to always turn your machine off when you switch cartridges. When you switch cartridges leaving the machine on it is called "hot swapping" and it can sometimes cause the machine to freeze. This is more of an issue with the older models and does not seem to apply to the Expression 2.

You know how quirky electronic gadgets can be, so give your machine a rest for five or ten minutes every hour. If you work for several hours continuously, your machine might overheat and freeze up.

Turn the machine off and take a break. Restart it when you come back, and it should be fine. Then remember not to rush programming the machine and give it an occasional rest.

Do not press a long list of commands quickly. If you give it too much information too quickly it will get confused in the same way a computer sometimes does and simply freeze up. Instead

of typing in one long phrase try dividing up your words into several cuts.

If you are using special feature keys make sure you press them first before selecting the letters.

Power Problems

If you turn your machine on and nothing happens the power adapter may be at fault. Jiggle the power cord at the outlet and where it connects to the machine to make sure it is firmly connected. Ideally, you want to test the adapter before buying a new one. Swap cords with a friend and see if that fixed the problem. Replacement adapters can be found on eBay by searching for Cricut adapter power supply.

The connection points inside the machine may also pose a problem; here is how to test that. Hold down the plug where it inserts into the back of the machine and turn it on. If it powers up, then the problem is inside the machine and the connection points will have to be soldered again.

If the machine powers up but will not cut, then try a hard reset. See the resource section for step-by-step instructions on resetting your machine.

Here are a few tips especially for Expression 2 users. Have you

turned on your machine, you watch it light up and hear it gearing up but when you try to cut nothing happens? Or you are stuck on the welcome screen or the LCD screen is unresponsive.

Well here are two quick fixes to try. First try a hard reset sometimes called the rainbow screen reset to recalibrate your die cutter. If that does not resolve the problem, you are going to have to restore the settings.

To help cut down on errors try to keep your machine updated. When an update is available, you should receive a message encouraging you to install the latest version.

For those of you using third party software that is no longer compatible with the Cricut you probably already know that updating your machine may disable that software.

When you cut heavy paper and your Expression 2 shuts down try switching to the normal paper setting and use the multi cut function.

Carriage Will Not Move

If the carriage assembly does not move, check to see if the belt has broken or if the car has fallen off the track. Provo Craft does not sell replacement parts, which is nuts, so try to find a

compatible belt at a vacuum repair shop.

If the wheels have fallen off the track, remove the plastic cover and look for a tiny screw by the wheel unscrew it. You now should be able to move the wheel back on track.

Unresponsive Keyboard

If you are sure you are pressing the keys firmly, you have a cartridge inserted correctly and a mat loaded ready to go, but the keypad is still not accepting your selection, the problem may be internal.

You will have to remove the keyboard and check if the display cable is connected to the keypad and to the motherboard. If the connections are secure, then you have a circuit board problem and repairs are beyond the scope of this book.

An important reminder, please do not attempt any repairs unless your machine is out of warranty.

Weird LCD Screen

The LCD screen is now showing strange symbols or is blank after doing a firmware update. Try running the update again making sure your selections are correct.

When the image you choose is bigger than the mat or paper

size you selected the preview screen will look grayed out instead of showing the image. So increase the paper and mat size or decrease the size of your image.

Also watch out for the gray box effect when using the center point feature. Move the start position down until you see the image appear. The same thing may happen when using the fit to length feature. Try changing to landscape mode and shorten the length size until the image appears.

Occasionally using the undo button will cause the preview screen to turn black; unfortunately, the only thing to do is turn the machine off. Your work will be lost, and you have to start again.

Cartridge Errors

Sometimes dust or debris accumulates in the cartridge port gently blow out any paper fiber that may have collected in the opening. Make sure the contact points are clean and that nothing is preventing the cartridge from being read properly.

With any electrical machine overheating can be a problem. If you get a cartridge error after using your machine for a while turn it off and let it cool down for about fifteen minutes.

If this is the very first time, you are using the cartridge and you

get an error I am sure you know the trick about turning the cartridge around and inserting it in backward.

If you thought you could use your Imagine cartridges with your Expression 2, think again. You will get an error message because you can only use the art cartridges that you can cut with, the colors and patterns cartridge are for printing.

Even brand-new items fresh out of the box can be defective. If you see a cartridge error 1, 2, 3, 4, 5, 6, 9 or 99 call customer service and tell them the name, serial number and error message number and they may replace the cartridge.

Trouble Connecting to Your Computer

All Cricut machines come with a USB cord that lets you connect to your computer and allows you to use the other products like the Cricut Design Studio software, Cricut Craft Room, or the Cricut Gypsy with your machines.

Double check your USB connection and try another port.

Check to see if you may have a firewall or antivirus software that is blocking the connection.

See if you are running the latest firmware. You may need to update. Older machines update via firmware (Personal Cutter, Expression, Create and Cake) the newer (Expression 2, Imagine and Gypsy) use the Sync program to update.

Chapter 7

How to Make Money with Cricut Machine

1. Dare to Be Different

You have to be yourself, unleash your quirkiness and creativity.

Those that have been in the Cricut crafts world for some time know all about the knockout name tiles. They became a hit and in no time, everyone was producing and selling them.

In the crafting world, that is the norm. Thus, you could be among the earliest people to jump on a trend to ride the wave until the next hot seller surfaces. Mind you, that strategy of selling Cricut crafts can become costly and tiresome if you are not careful.

The basic idea here is to add your flair and personal style, and not to completely re-invent the wheel. For example, let us say you come across two name tiles on Etsy, one looks exactly like the other 200+ on sale on the site, while the second one has a few more tweaks and spins on it. The seller of the second product will possibly charge more and accrue a higher profit because his/her product is unique and stands out from the rest.

Whe n you design your products, do not be afraid to tweak your fonts, because even the simplest of tweaks and creativity can make your product stand out from the rest.

Remember this; if you create a product that looks exactly like others, you are only putting yourself in a 'price war', where no one usually wins.

2. Keep It Narrow

A lot of crafters out there believe that creating and selling everything under the sun translates into more patronage, and more money, but that is not how it works. On the contrary, it might only result in a huge stock of unsold products, more burn out and heavy cost. Rather than producing materials here and there, you should focus on being the best in your area of craftiness, so that when people need specific products in your area, they will come to you.

It can be very tempting to want to spread your tentacles because it might seem like the more you produce, the more options you will provide for your clients, but that might be counterproductive.

Take out time to think about your area of strength and focus your energy on making products that you would be known for. It is better to be known as an expert in a particular product than to be renowned for someone that produces a high number of inferior products.

Thus, you should keep it narrow and grow to become the very best in your area of craft.

3. Be Consistent

If you intend to become successful, you have to consistently work on your Cricut craft business. Some people work once a week or thereabout because they sell as a hobby; however, if you intend to make in-road in your business, you have to work every day.

If you have other engagements and cannot work every day, then you should create a weekly schedule and stick to it. If you shun your business for weeks and months at a time, then you will not go anywhere with it.

Apart from consistency in work and production, you also have to be consistent with your product quality and pricing. When your customers are convinced about your products, they will easily recommend you to their friends, family, business partners, and many others.

In business, there are ups and downs, thus, you should not reduce your work rate because things are not going as planned. Success does not come easy, but one of the surest ways of being and maintaining success is by consistently doing the things you love.

4. Be Tenacious

It is not easy to run a business because it involves a lot of hard work, sweat, and even heartbreaks. Thus, you have to bear in mind that there will be days when you will feel like throwing in the towel. There will be days when nothing goes as planned. There will also be days when customers will tick you off. You will feel like a drowning boat because you are working hard but nothing is working out.

However, you have to look at the bigger picture, because the crafting business is not a get rich quick scheme. Remember, quitters never win, so quitting is not an option. Keep doing the things you love and keep improving. Successful people never give up. They suffer many setbacks, but they do not stop.

Thus, for you to be successful in your craft, you have to be tenacious and resilient. Be willing to maneuver your way through tough times, and do not forget to pick up lessons.

5. Learn Everyday

Be willing to learn from people that have been successful in the business. You do not necessarily have to unravel everything by yourself, because whatever it is you are doing, others have already done it in the past.

Whether you intend to learn how to build a successful Facebook group or how to go up the Etsy ranks, remember that people have already done all that in the past, and are giving out tricks and tips they know.

Make it a tradition to learn something new about your business every day because, at the beginning of your business, you will have to do more marketing than crafting.

When you wake up in the morning, browse through the internet, gather materials, and read at your spare time, because the more you learn the better your chances of being successful. They say knowledge is power, and for you to become successful as a craftsman/woman, you have to constantly seek new knowledge in the form of tips, tricks, software upgrades, marketing, design ideas, tools, accessories, and many others.

All I am saying is that you should learn without ceasing.

6. Quality Control

If you intend to grow your brand, you must prioritize the selling of high-quality products. Your motto should quality over everything.

For you to easily succeed, people should know you as someone that sells top quality products, because quality wins over quantity every day of the week.

You do not want to be known as someone that produces poor quality items because when the word spreads (and it surely will), your business will pack up.

If you focus your attention and efforts on the production of high-quality materials, you will be able to withstand competition, no matter how stiff it is.

7. Think About A Coach

Business mentors are extremely popular nowadays. Consider going through some cash with a Scrapbooking business mentor who comprehends the business as well as genuinely comprehends the specific brand of energy scrapbook sweethearts share. A mentor can help share business abilities however can go about as an extraordinary coach in managing you to your objectives.

It is more than conceivable to transform your energy into benefits. In the event that you do, you will never be motivated to consider your workday the everyday routine. Instead, you will discover achievement, motivation, and genuine satisfaction!

8. Exhibit Your True Talent with A Business Card for Artists

The financial downturn has left vast numbers of us feeling the squeeze. Numerous individuals are searching for approaches to set aside cash in each part of life. Be that as it may, there are times when a buy must be made, and careful research regularly structures some portion of the necessary leadership the procedure. For the individuals who have their own business, these can be precarious occasions undoubtedly, so it could really compare to ever to make your business stick out. In the event that you are associated with the craftsmanship world, a fantastic method to acquaint yourself with potential clients is through a business card for artisans.

9. Give the Quality of Your Work A Chance to Radiate Through

A business card for specialists is your window to the world, and it should say a great deal regarding your aesthetic edge and abilities. Make it state every little thing about you and what you can offer. Plan a motivating logo that can join the substance of what you can do with an incredible structure. This astute connecting can put you on top of things by helping individuals to recollect who and what you are.

10. Consider Other Ways You Can Display Your Skills to The World

A business card for specialists is only one of numerous limited time apparatuses you can use to enhance your presentation. It bodes well. The production of a notice is an excellent method to demonstrate the best of what you do. Try not to place a lot into your sign; that will go about as an obstacle and prevent individuals from getting a vibe of your actual abilities. Consider the area where you can show your blurb. Vital arranging of the setting of your sign can help augment its effect. It will expand the intrigue of your work and open up more potential outcomes.

11. Remember to Tell Individuals How to Connect!

A business card for specialists needs not exclusively to demonstrate the embodiment of your innovativeness; it likewise fills a need. It needs to tell potential clients how to connect with you. Incorporate all the distinctive contact techniques you have, email, site, telephone numbers, and any online networking you are an individual from. Remember about the intensity of internet-based life and bookmarking destinations; they can enable feature to considerably a more significant amount of your work.

12. Be Adaptable

Consider chipping away at zones that you had not imagined, however will be something inside your abilities. This will enable you to set up a notoriety. Another viable method to advance your aptitudes notwithstanding utilizing a business card for specialists is to engage in network ventures where you offer your administrations for nothing. Make something stunning that individuals will see every day; this is an incredible advert for your aptitudes. This will place your work into the lives of thousands of individuals and will drive more clients to you.

Chapter 8

Cricut Vocabulary, Tips, Tricks, Keyboard Shortcuts, and Selling Your Crafts

Now that you are more familiar with Design Space and the Cricut machines, you may have come across a few terms you were not familiar with. This Chapter lists some of the common Cricut terminology, a few Design Space tips and tricks, as well as some pointers on selling your crafts.

Cricut Vocabulary

When working with the Cricut cutting machines and Design Space, you are going to come across different terminology. The following is a glossary of the Cricut vocabulary to help you better understand the system.

Backing

Backing is the back sheet of material such as vinyl. It is the part of the material that gets stuck onto the cutting mat and is usually the last part of the material to be removed after cutting, weeding, and transfer of the project.

Bleed

The bleed refers to a space around each item to be cut. This gives the cutting machine the ability to make a more precise cut. It is a small border that separates cutting elements on a page. This option can be turned off, but it is not recommended.

Bonded Fabric

Bonded fabric is material that is not very elastic, it is held together with adhesive and is not patterned woven type fabric.

Blade

Cricut has a few different types of cutting blades and tips. Each leaf has its own unique function enabling it to cut various materials.

Blade Housing

The blade housing is the cylindrical tube that holds the blade and fits into the blade head and blade accessory compartment of the Cricut cutting machine.

Blank

Cricut offers items, called blanks, to use with various projects for vinyl, iron-on, heat transfer vinyl, or infusible ink. These items include T-shirts, tote bags, coasters, and baby onesies.

Brayer

The Brayer is a tool that looks a bit like a lint roller brush. It is used to flatten and stick material or objects down smoothly as it irons out bubbles, creases, etc.

Bright Pad

A Bright Pad is a device that looks like a tablet. This device has a strong backlight to light up materials to help with weeding and defining intricate cuts. It is a convenient tool to have and can be used for other DIY projects as well.

Butcher Paper

Butcher paper is the white paper that comes with the Cricut Infusible Inks sheets. It is used to act as a barrier between the EasyPress or iron when transferring the ink sheet onto a blank or item.

Carriage

The carriage is the bar in the Cricut cutting machine which the blade moves across.

Cartridge

Cartridges are what the older models of the Cricut cutting machine used to cut images. Each round would hold a set of images. They can still be used with the Cricut Explore Air 2 which has a docking site for them. If you want to use them with a Cricut Maker, you will have to buy the USB adaptor. Design Space still supports the use of Cartridge images.

Cartridges also come in a digital format.

Cricut Maker Adaptive Tool System

The Cricut Maker comes with an advanced tools system control using intricate brass gears. These new tools have been designed to aid the machine in making precise cuts and being able to cut more materials such as wood, metal, and leather.

Cut Lines

These are the lines along which the cutting machine will cut out the project's shapes.

Cutting Mat

There are a few different types of cutting mats also known as machine mats. Most of the large rugs can be used on both the Cricut Explore Air 2 and the Cricut Maker. The Cricut Joy needs mats that are designed specifically for it.

Cut Screen

When you are creating projects in Design Space, there is a green button on the top right-hand corner of the screen called the Make it button. When the project is ready to be cut, this button is clicked on. Once that button has been clicked, the user is taken to another screen where they will see how the project is going to be cut out. This is the Cut Screen.

Drive Housing

The Drive Housing is different from the Blade Housing in that it has a gold wheel at the top of the blade. These blades can only be used with the Cricut Maker cutting machine.

EasyPress

A Cricut EasyPress is a handheld pressing iron that is used for iron-on, heat transfer vinyl (HTV), and infusible ink. The EasyPress' latest models are the EasyPress 2 and the EasyPress Mini.

EasyPress Mat

There are a few different EasyPress Mat sizes that are available on the market. These mats make transferring iron-on, heat transfer vinyl, and infusible ink a lot simpler. These mats should be used for these applications instead of an ironing board to ensure the project's success.

Firmware

Firmware is a software patch, update, or new added functionality for a device. For cutting machines it would be new drivers updates, cutting functionality, and so on. Both Design Space software, Cricut cutting machines, and Cricut EasyPress 2 machines need to have their Firmware updated on a regular basis.

Go Button

This can also be called the "Cut" button. This is the button on the Cricut cutting or EasyPress machine that has the green Cricut "C" on it. It is the button that is pressed when a project is ready to be cut or pressed for the EasyPress models.

JPG File

A JPG file is a common form of digital image. These image files can be uploaded for use with a Design Space project.

Kiss Cut

When the cutting machine cuts through the material but not the material backing sheet it is called a Kiss Cut.

Libraries

Libraries are lists of images, fonts, or projects that have been uploaded by the user or maintained by Cricut Design Space.

PNG File

A PNG file is another form of a graphics (image) file. It is most commonly used in Web-based graphics for line drawings, small graphic/icon images, and text.

Ready to Make Projects

Design Space contains ready to make projects which are projects that have already been designed. All the user has to do is choose the plan to load in Design Space, get the material ready, and then Make it to cut the design out. These projects can be customized as well.

Scraper Tool

The Scraper tool comes in small and large. It is used to make sure material sticks firmly to a cutting mat, object, or transfer sheet.

Self-Healing Mat

Cricut has many handy accessories and tools to help with a person's crafting. One of these helpful tools is the Self-Healing Mat. This mat is not for use in a cutting machine but can be used with handheld slicing tools to cut material to exact specifications

SVG File

The SVG file format is the most common format for graphic files in Cricut Design Space. This is because these files can be manipulated without losing their quality.

Transfer Sheet/Paper

A transfer sheet or transfer paper is a sheet that is usually clear and has a sticky side. These sheets are used to transfer various materials like transfer vinyl, sticker sheets, and so on onto an item.

Weeding/Reverse Weeding

Weeding is the process of removing vinyl or material from a cut pattern or design that has been left behind after removing the excess content. For example, weeding the middle of the letter "O" to leave the middle of it hollow.

Reverse Weeding would be leaving the middle of the letter "O" behind and removing the outside of it.

Weeding Tool

The Weeding tool has a small hooked head with a sharp point. This tool is used to pick off the material that is not needed on a cut. For instance, when cutting out the letter 'O' the weeding tool is used to remove the middle of the message so that it is hollow. Cleaning up a cut design with the Weeding tool is called weeding.

Design Space Tips and Tricks

This section covers a few tips and tricks to help you master Design Space.

Keyboard Shortcuts

The following are a few useful keyboard shortcuts that can be used in Design Space:

Copy — Ctrl+C

Paste — Ctrl+V

Cut — Shift+Delete

Undo — Ctrl+Z

A Few Design Space Tips

Here are a few handy tips for Navigating Design Space:

Color Sync Panel

To match up object colors quickly and accurately or cut down on material colors, use the Color Sync Panel. This panel is also handy to use for exactly matching non-standard colors.

Search Bar

When searching for Images, Fonts, or Projects you will get more choices if you clearly define your search. For instance, if you are searching for Roses leave off the 's' and search for Rose instead. If you are searching for elephants choose the Animal or Wildlife categories and then search for elephant.

Canvas Workspace

To change the look of the Workspace without using the Main menu Setting options, click in the blank space between the X and Y axis ruler at the top left-hand corner of the page. This will reset the Grid.

Save Most Used Materials

Instead of searching through hundreds of Material options when you are ready to cut out the design, add your most used materials to Favorites.

Use Selected Objects Functions

When you select an object on the Workspace screen or on the Prepare screen, you will notice a box surrounding the selected item. The box will have icons on either all four box corners or two of the box corners. Those are quick shortcut keys for Delete, Rotate, Move, Hide, Size, and Unlock an object.

Selling Your Cricut Craft for Profit

If you are a severe crafter you are going to want to sell your Cricut crafts. You can sell the crafts you make with your Cricut cutting machines. As long as you do not use Licensed Images from the Cricut Library, most of the other fonts, images, and projects can be used with crafts you wish to sell.

Is There a Market for Cricut Crafts?

There certainly is a market for any homemade crafts. Especially ones that look professional, which the polish the Cricut cutting machines and superior materials give the finished product.

Popular Cricut Items

There are lots of different items a person can make with Cricut cutting machines that sell really well. Some of these items include:

- Personalized vinyl decals for walls, mirrors, windows, cutlery, crockery, jars, etc.

- Iron-on logos and images for cushions, tea-towels, clothing, curtains, hats, trainers, etc.

- Leather jewelry, clutch bags, cushions, etc.

- Dog collars and dog tags

- Welcome mats

- Personalized mugs, tumblers, glasses, and electronic devices

  - Signs

- Business cards

- Greeting cards

  - Envelops

- Gift boxes

- Decorations and banners

Where to Sell Cricut Items

You can sell Craft items on your own personal website, social media sites, sites like Etsy, Amazon, and eBay.

Chapter 9

Maintenance of the Cricut Machine

Every Cricut machine needs to be cleaned and taken care of in order to keep it working for as long as possible. Here, you will learn about the maintenance required for Cricut machines, and what you can do to keep your computer working efficiently.

Cleaning and Care

Cleaning your machine is very important, and you should do it regularly to keep everything in tip-top shape. If you do not take care of your device, that's just money down the drain.

But what can you do to care for your machine? Well, I do suggest initially that you make sure to run maintenance on it as much as you can and keep it clean. There are a few other tips and tricks that can help prolong the machine's life. For starters, keep liquids and food away from the device – never drink or eat while you use your Cricut machine. Set up your device in a location that is free of dust and try to keep it away from excessive coolness or heat, so do not just throw it in the attic or an especially cold basement. If you are transporting your machine to use it at a different location, never leave it in the car. Excessive heat will melt the machine's plastic components, so be careful.

Finally, make sure the machine is stored away from sunlight. Keep it out of places in the home where sunlight hits it directly. For example, if you have an office that is very bright and the sun warms the machine for a long period of time, you will want to move it so that it does not get damaged.

Be gentle with your machine. Remember, it is a machine, so you will want to make sure that you do take some time and try to keep it nice and in order. Do not be rough with it, and when working with the machine parts, do not be too rough with them, either.

Caring for your machine is not just about making sure that the parts do not get dirty, but you should also make sure that you keep everything in good working order.

Cleaning the Machine Itself

In general, the exterior is pretty easy to clean – you just need a damp cloth. Use a soft cloth to wipe it off, and keep in mind that chemical cleaners with benzene, acetone, or carbon tetrachloride should never be used on your Cricut machine. Any cleaner that is scratchy, as well, should be avoided at all costs.

Make sure that you never put any machine components in water. This should be obvious, but often, people may use a piece of a damp cloth, thinking that it will be fine when in reality, it is not.

You should consider getting some non-alcoholic wipes for cleaning your machine. Always disconnect the power before cleaning, as you would with any machine. The Cricut machine can then be lightly wiped down. Some people also use a glass cleaner sprayed on a cloth but do be careful to make sure no residue builds up. If you notice there is some dust there, you can typically get away with a cloth that is soft and clean.

Sometimes, grease can build up – you may notice this on the cartridge bar if you use cartridges a lot. Use a swab of cotton or a soft cloth to remove it.

Greasing the Machine

If you need to grease your machine, first make sure that it is turned off and the smart carriage is moved to the left. Use a tissue to wipe this down, and then move it to the right, repeating the process again.

From there, move the carriage to the center and open up a lubrication package. Put a small amount onto a Q-tip. Apply a thin coating, greasing everything evenly, and also clean any buildup that may have occurred. This is usually the issue if you hear grinding noise when cleaning the machine itself.

There are a few other important places that you should make sure to clean, besides the outside and the carriage. Any places where blades are should be cleaned; you can just move the housing unit of the blade to clean it. You should also check the drawing area, to make sure there is not any excessive ink there.

Never use spray cleaner directly on the machine, for obvious reasons. The bar holding the housing should not be wiped down, but if you do notice an excessive grease, please take the time to make sure that it is cleaned up. Remember to never touch the gear chain near the back of this unit, either, or never clean with the machine on, for your own safety.

When caring for a Cricut machine, try to do this more frequently if you are using the machine a lot, or twice yearly. If you notice strange noises coming from the machine, do get a grease packet. You can always contact Cricut and they will help you figure out the issue, if there is one, with your machine.

Cricut machines are great, but you need to take care in making sure that you keep everything in rightful order.

Cutting Blade

Your blades will tend to dull over time, but this is usually a very slow process. The best way to prevent it is to have different blades to cut different materials. Having a different blade for each material is a really good idea.

You can get fine-point ones which are good for smaller items; deep-cut, which is great for leather and other fabrics; bonded fabric, so great for fabric pieces; a rotary blade for those heavy fabrics; and finally, a knife blade, which is good for those really thick items.

In order to maintain your blades, you should clean the housing area for every blade after each use, since they get gunky fast. Squirting compressed air into the area is a wonderful way to get the dust out of there.

As for the blades, remember foil? Use a little bit of that over the edges of the blade to help clean and polish them up. To polish them, you should put them on the cutting mat and from there, cut small designs on it. It actually does help with sharpening them, and it does not require you to completely remove them. You can do this with every single blade, too!

To change the blades in their housings, just open the clamps, pull up, and remove the housing within the machine. Put a new blade in, and then close it. That is all it takes.

Storing them is also pretty simple. There is a drop-down doorway at the front area of the machine. It is made for storing the blades within their housings. Put your loose blades in there first, then utilize the magnet to keep them in place. The best part about this storage is that your blades are always with the Cricut, even if you take the machine somewhere else.

There is also a blade organizer that you can use, too, made out of chipboard with some holders attached. This is also a wonderful means to store all of your items. Organizing your Cricut blades is very important, and understanding the best places to keep them is, of course, essential.

Cutting Mat

Your cutting mats need to be cleaned because if you do not clean them frequently, they will attract dirt and lose adhesiveness. That means you will have to spend more money on mats, which is not ideal. There are different ways to clean them, and we will go over a few of the different means to clean your mats so you can use them for longer.

Cleaning the Mat Itself

First, if your mat is completely filthy, you need to clean it. Of course, you will also want to do this for just general maintenance, too. Once it has been cleaned, you will notice it is sticky again.

Typically, washing it down with either a magic eraser or a kitchen scrubber can do it. Sometimes, if it is really dirty, you might want to get some rubbing alcohol onto a wipe. If you notice a chunk of the debris left behind, however, is fabric oriented, then get some lint rollers or even just stick some scotch tape on there and pull it off. This can eliminate the issue.

But what about the really tough grime? Well, get some Goo Gone cleaner. Put a little bit on the troublesome spots and wipe it around, and then let the goo stick on there. From there, get an old card or something to get it off, and then wash the mat. Once it is dry, check to see if it is sticky. If it is, then great – you do not need to do anything more. But what if you notice that it is still not sticky? Well, why not restick the cutting mat itself!

Resticking The Mat

To do this, you need to make sure that you tape the edges, so you do not get adhesive near the edges, and mess with the rollers of the machine. Once that is there, use either spray adhesive or glue stick, and then let it dry. If you notice that it is still not sticky enough when you are finished applying the first coat, apply a second coat.

There are great adhesives out there, such as simple spray adhesive, easy tack, quilt basting, bonding, and also repositionable e glue. All of these are fairly effective, and if you notice that the mat is actually sticking pretty well, then you are in luck.

However, always make sure that you let this fully dry. If you do not let the adhesive dry and you start using the mat again, you will run into the problem of the material being stuck to it.

Once it is dried, try it out with some test material. If you find it too sticky at this point, but either your hands or a shirt on there to help reduce the tackiness.

Caring for Machines and Mats

Here are a couple of other tips to use with your cutting mats.

The first, use different mats. You may notice that you can get more out of one type of mat than another kind, which is something many people do not realize. Often, if you notice that you get a lot more out of the firmer grip mats, buy more of those.

Finally, halve your mats. You can save immensely by making sure that they are cut in half. This does work, and it helps pretty well.

You can expect anywhere from about 25 to 40 different cuts before you will need to replace the mat, but cleaning after about half of that can definitely help with improving the quality of your cuts. The life of the mat, of course, does vary based on the settings and what materials you cut. When you cannot get it to stick, try cleaning and resticking it, but if you notice that it is still not doing the job, you are going to need to get a replacement.

Taking care of your Cricut machine will get you more use out of it, so make sure you perform regular maintenance on all your machine's components so it can be used for years.

Chapter 10

Advanced Tips and Tricks

L earning to use the "Cricut" machine definitely involves a steep learning curve. The more complicated aspect of it all is using the "Design Space" software to hone down a variety of features and tools to help you craft your designs and turn your "inspiration into creation". There are multiple shortcuts on the "Design Space" application to make your designing not only easy but more efficient. Let us look at some of the tips and tricks that will make your creative self-stronger and happier!

"Design Space" application

• The "Weld", "Contour" and "Slice" functionalities to customize your designs. These 3 tools will be activated at the bottom of the screen for designs that allow for these changes.

• The "Weld" tool will allow you to merge two different designs to obtain one composite design, without any leftover seams and cut lines that might be present on the individual designs. This helps in obtaining single continuous cut for your design, so you do not need to glue and assemble multiple pieces to obtain the final design, for example, creation of cake toppers, gift tags and other decorations.

• The "Contour" tool can be used to activate or deactivate any cut lines in any cut files and thereby allowing you to customize the image in various ways. So imagine you have an image of a flower and you want to remove the details of the design and obtain more of an outline of the flower, you can do so by clicking on the "Contour" button at the bottom of the screen and selecting the different elements of the image that you want to turn on or off from the contour pop-up window.

• The "Slice" tool can be used to slice a design from an image by cutting out or removing elements of the image, as shown in the picture below.

• Use your search keywords wisely. The search functionality within the "Design Space" is not very dynamic so your choice of keywords will make a big difference on the designs and projects that will be displayed to you. For example, if you search for images containing dotted designs and search with keyword "Dots", you would be given around 120 images but if you search with the term "Dot" you would see almost twice as many images. You should also search with synonyms and closely related terms of your target project idea. For instance, if you wanted to create a Halloween project, you can search with terms like pumpkin, costumes and trick or treat, among others. This will ensure you are viewing any and all images pertaining to your project.

• The "Cartridge" image sets. It is likely that during your search, you like a design more than any other made available to you but it is not exactly how you want it to be. Well, simply click on the small information circle (i) at the bottom of the image and you will be able to view the entire image set or "cartridge" of images similar to your selected image within the "Design Space Image Library".

• A treasure trove of free fonts and images. As a beginner you would want to utilize a large number of free fonts and images to get your hands-on experience with your "Cricut" device. This is a great way to spend less money and still be able to create stunning craft projects. Within the "Design Space" application, you can click on the "Filter" icon next to the search bar (available within the images, fonts, and projects tabs) and select "Free" to only view free resources within each category.

• Use synchronized colors to save time and money. This is a great tool when you have designs that are either a composite of multiple images or inherently contains different hues of the same color. Instead of using 5 different shades of the same color, you can synchronize the colors, so you need to use only one colored sheet. To do this, simply click on the "Color Sync" tab on the "Layers Panel" on the top right corner of the screen. Then drag and drop desired layer(s) of the design to your target color layer and the moved layer will immediately be modified to have the same color as the target color.

• Use the "Hide" tool to selectively cut images from the Canvas. When you are looking to turn your imagination into a work of art, you may want to view and take inspirations from multiple images while you work on your design. But once you obtain your desired design you would not want to cut every other image on your canvas. This is where the "Hide" tool comes in handy, so you do not need to delete the images on the Canvas to avoid cutting them along with your project design. To hide the image, you just need to click on the "eye" symbol next to those specific image layers on the "Layers Panel". The hidden images will not be deleted from the Canvas but would not appear on the cutting mat when you click the "Make It" button to cut your project.

• Ability to change the design lines to be cut, scored or drawn. With the latest version of the "Design Space" application, you have the ability to simply change the "Linetype" of a design from its predefined type to your desired action, instead of looking for designs that have predefined line type meeting your project need. For example, if your selected design is set at "Linetype" Cut but you want the design to be "Linetype" Score, you can easily change the "Linetype" by clicking on the "Linetype" drop-down and making your selection.

• The power of the "Pattern" tool. You can use your own uploaded images to be used as pattern fill for your designs. Moreover, you will also be able to edit the image pattern and the patterns that already exist within the "Design Space" application to create your own unique and customized patterns. The "Edit Pattern" window allows you to adjust the resolution and positioning of the pattern on your design and much more. (Remember, to use the "Pattern" feature you must use the "Print then Cut" approach for your project, with access to a printer).

• Utilize the standard "keyboard shortcuts". The "Design Space" application does have all the required tools and buttons to allow you to edit the images and fonts but if you prefer to use your keyboard shortcuts to quickly edit the image, the "Design Space" application will support that. Some of the keyboard shortcuts you can use include: "Copy (Control + C)"; "Paste (Control + V)"; "Delete (Delete key)"; "Copy (Control + Z)".

• You can utilize the "Slice" tool to crop the image. The "Design Space" application still lacks the "Crop" functionality, so if you need to crop an image, you will need to get creative. A good tip is to use the "Slice" tool along with the "Shapes" to get your desired image.

• Change the position of the design on the cutting Mat. When you are ready to cut your design and click on the "Make It" button, you will notice that your design will be aligned on the top left corner of the mat. Now, if you are using material that was priorly cut at its top left corner, you can simply drag and move the image on the "Design Space" mat to meet the positioning of your cutting material. You will be able to cut the image anywhere on the mat by moving the design on that specific position on the mat.

• Moving design from one mat to the another. Yes! You can not only move the design over the mat itself, you can also move the design from one mat to another by simply clicking on the three dots (…) on top of the mat and select "Move to another mat". You will then view a pop-up window where you can select from the existing mats for your project to be used as the new mat for your selected design.

• Save cut materials as Favorites for quick access. Instead of spending time filtering and searching for your cut material on the "Design

Space" application over and over, just save your frequently used material by clicking on the star next to the "Cricut" logo on the "Design Space" application to save them under the "Favorites" tab next to the default "All Materials" tab. When you are getting ready to cut your project, under the "Set Material" tab, your "Favorites" material will be displayed on the screen, as shown in the picture below.

• You can store the most frequently used cut materials on the "Cricut Maker". Unlike the "Cricut Explore" series which has dial settings for a variety of commonly used cut materials, the "Cricut Maker" requires you to use a "Custom Materials" menu within the "Design Space" application that can be accessed using the button on the machine bearing "Cricut" logo, since there is no dial to choose the material you want to cut.

• Choose to repeat the cut of the same mat or skip a mat from being cut altogether. By following the instructions on the "Design Space" and feeding the right color and size of the material to the machine, you will be able to get your design perfectly cut. You can change the order in which the mats are cut, repeat the cut of your desired mat, and even skip cutting a mat, if needed. You can do this easily by simply clicking on and selecting the mat you would like to cut.

• You can edit the cut settings your materials. You might notice that even when you have selected the default settings to cut the desired material, the material may not cut as desired. To help with this, "Design Space" allows you to adjust the cut settings for all the materials such as the depth of the cut, the cutting blade and the number of the passes to be made by the "Cricut" device. Since this may not be as intuitive to most beginners, here is a step by step walkthrough of this process:

1. When using the "Cricut Maker", select "Materials" on the cut screen and if using the "Cricut Explore" series, set the dial to "Custom".

2. Click on "Browse All Materials" from the top of the menu.

3. From the bottom of the screen, select "Material Settings".

4. The pop-up window for the "Custom Materials" will be displayed as shown in the picture below, where you can make the required adjustments.

• Adjust the pressure with which the material can be cut. You may want to just adjust the pressure with which the cut is made to obtain clean and neat cut of the material, without needing to go through the process described above to adjust the cut setting of the material. On the cut screen, once you have selected the cut material, a drop-down option with "Default" setting will be displayed. Simply click on the drop-down button and adjust pressure to "More" or "Less".

• "Cricut Access Membership" – At a monthly fee of around $8 or an annual membership fee, you will be able to use a larger variety of fonts and imaged for free. You will be able to freely use more than 30K images, over 370 fonts and thousands of projects saving a lot of money in the long run, depending on your usage.

Chapter 11

FAQs

1.   Where can I use Cricut Design Space?

You can use Cricut Design Space through your web browser on PC or Mac after downloading the plugin. You can also download the app on your tablet or smartphone on iOS or Android.

2.   How does my machine connect to Design Space?

Explore Air 2 has built-in Bluetooth, so it can connect to any device that has that capability. The Explore One has to be connected directly to your computer, or you can purchase a Cricut Wireless Bluetooth Adapter.

3.   What is Cricut Access?

This is Cricut's subscription service to their library of images and fonts in Cricut Design Space. It gives access to more than 30,000 images, 370 fonts, and premium project ideas, as well as 10% off all purchases on the Cricut website. There are different types of plans available, ranging from $4.99 to $9.99 per month.

4.   How do I install Design Space?

Open your web browser and enter design.cricut.com into the address bar. After signing in, select New Project. Design Space will give you a prompt to download and install the plugin. Click Download and wait for it to finish. Once it does, click the file to install the plugin. You might get a box asking for permission; if so, allow it. Follow the prompts through the installer. You are now ready to use Design Space!

5.   Why am I getting error messages about the Design Space plugin?

If you are getting error messages or having difficulty using Design Space, you may need to reinstall the plugin. Expand your computer's system tray in the lower right-hand side of the screen and locate the Cricut icon. Right-click on it and click Exit. Open your web browser and navigate to design.cricut.com and sign in with your Cricut ID. Once prompted, download, and install the plugin again.

6.   Do I need a computer to use my Cricut machine?

No! If you have the Cricut Explore Air or the Cricut Maker, you can utilize the built-in Bluetooth to connect to your mobile device and download the Design Space app on it.

7.   What is the difference between the Cricut Explore One and the Cricut Explore Air 2?

The Cricut Explore One has a single tool carriage, so if you do more than one action (cut and write or cut and score), it will need to do it in two steps, and you'll need to switch out the tools between them. The Cricut Explore Air 2 has two tool carriages, so it can do both functions in one step with no need to switch tools. Explore Air 2 also has built-in Bluetooth connectivity.

8.   Do I use the same Cricut Design Space for the Cricut Maker?

Yes! The only difference is that you will have the option to adjust the material settings in the Design Space since the Maker does not have the dial on the machine itself.

9.   How does the Cricut Maker know which blade is in the carriage?

The machine scans the blade before it cuts a project.

10.   What is the thickness of a material that the Cricut Maker can cut?

3/32" of an inch or 2.4mm when using the rotary blade or the knife blade.

11.   How do I get a good transfer using the Cricut EasyPress?

Use the EasyPress on a firm and even surface. Check the iron-on material and the base material for the recommended settings and use those. Be sure to apply heat to both the front and back of the project for the recommended amount of time.

12.   How much pressure does the Cricut EasyPress need?

Check the recommendations for the material you are using. Some will call for "firm" pressure, meaning you should use two hands and about 15–20 lbs of body weight. Others need "gentle" pressure, meaning you should use one hand with about 5–10 lbs of body weight. Use your EasyPress on a waist-high table for the easiest way to apply pressure.

13.   Do I move the Cricut EasyPress around like an iron?

Keep the EasyPress in one spot for the recommended amount of time. Moving it might smear or warp the design.

14.   Why should I use the Cricut EasyPress?

It heats more evenly and more quickly than iron and is easy to use. It will give you more professional-looking iron-ons and takes 60 seconds or less.

15.   How do I protect surfaces while using the Cricut EasyPress?

Cricut recommends using the Cricut EasyPress mat, which comes in three different sizes. However, you can also use a cotton bath towel with an even texture folded to about 3 inches thick. Do not use an ironing board, as the surface is not even enough, and it is too unsteady to apply appropriate pressure. Silicone baking mats and aluminum foil do not provide enough insulation and can get dangerously hot.

16.   My material is tearing! Why?

The most common reason is that your mat is not sticky enough. It could have lost its stickiness, or you are not using the right mat for the material. It could also be that the blade needs to be replaced or sharpened, or you are using the wrong type of blade. Materials can also tear if the machine is on the wrong setting.

17.   Why won't my transfer tape work?

More often than not, it is not working when you try to use standard transfer tape with glitter vinyl. It requires the Cricut Strong Grip transfer tape. It is too strong to use with regular vinyl, though, so keep using the regular transfer tape for that.

18.   What type of mat should I use?

Each mat has a specific use. Here is each one and some suggestions of what material to use with them.

•   Blue: Light Grip Mat – Thinner paper, vellum, construction paper, sticky notes, light vinyl, and wrapping paper

•   Green: Standard Grip Mat – Cardstock, thicker paper, washi paper, plastic, and bonded fabric

•   Purple: Strong Grip Mat – Thick cardstock, magnet sheets, chipboard, poster board, fabric with stiffener, aluminum foil, foam, leather, and suede

•   Pink: Fabric Grip Mat – Fabric, bonded fabric, and crepe paper

19.   How do I wash my mats?

Place the mat in the sink, supported by a firm flat surface. Running lukewarm water over it, use a hard-bristled brush to scrub it gently in circles until the mat is clean. Pat dry with a paper towel, and let it air dry for the stickiness to return.

20.   Why won't my blade cut all the way through the material?

Make sure that the blade is entirely in the carriage, and make sure there is no debris around it. Check that your settings are for the correct material. If you are still having trouble, slowly increase the pressure and do test cuts until it gets all the way through.

21.   Can I upload my own images to the Cricut Design Space?

Yes! It is easy to upload your own image and create a design with it. On the left side of Design Space, there is an option for "Upload Images."

22.   What is infusible ink?

Infusible ink is a new system from Cricut that infuses ink directly into compatible Cricut blanks. There are infusible ink transfer sheets and infusible ink Pens and Markers. They are applied using heat, such as with the Cricut EasyPress.

24.   Does Cricut Design Space require an internet connection?

Yes.

25.   What weight is Cricut Cardstock?

80 lb

26.   What are the care instructions for Cricut Iron-on material?

Wash and dry the item inside out on the delicate style. If you notice areas of the iron-on material coming off after being washed, iron it again, following the full application instructions.

27.   What is a quick reference list of materials I can cut?

For the Explore machines: all paper, all cardstock, vinyl, bonded fabrics, corrugated paper, sticker paper, and parchment paper. For the Maker machine: all of the above, plus material and textiles and thin wood.

28.   Do I have to use Cricut brand materials?

No! You can use any brand of materials that you want. Thickness and quality are the only things that matter.

29.   What pens can I use in my Cricut machine?

The Cricut brand pens will, of course, fit into your machine. However, some others will fit in the pen holder as well. Some users have found ways to adapt other pens, but the pens and markers in the following list do not require any adjustments.

•   Wal-Mart Leisure Arts Markers

•   Target Dual Tip Markers

- Pilot Precise V5 pens

- Thin Crayola markers

- Dollar Tree Jot markers

- Bic Round Stic pen

30.   What is the Cricut Adaptive Tool System?

This is a new feature in the Cricut Maker. It adjusts the direction and pressure of the blades throughout the cutting process. It allows for much more precise cuts and much higher cutting pressure.

31.   What is the difference between the different blades?

- Fine Point Blade – This is the blade that comes in the box with all of the machines. It is made of German Carbide. It is designed to cut medium-weight materials, including printer paper, vinyl, cardstock, washi tape, parchment paper, vellum, canvas, light chipboard, and very thin faux leather.

- Deep Point Blade – This blade is made for thicker materials and has a steeper angle—60 degrees—instead of the Fine Point's 45 degrees. It can cut craft foam, aluminum foil, genuine leather, metallic leather, magnetic sheet, and corrugated paper.

- Bonded Fabric Blade – This is for use exclusively on bonded fabric. A bonded fabric has a backing, such as Heat and Bond, adhered to it. Without the backing, the fabric will tear and stretch, and it may damage your mat. It can cut the bonded forms of oilcloth, silk, polyester, denim, felt, burlap, and cotton.

- Rotary Blade – This blade is only for the Cricut Maker and is included in the box. It utilizes the Adaptive Tool System. It can cut fabric without it being bonded. The materials you cut with this blade should be at least ¾ of an inch or 19mm thick, so as not to damage the blade. It can cut all fabric, including bamboo fabric, bengaline, canvas, cashmere, chiffon, corduroy, cotton, denim, felt, fleece, gauze, silk, lycra, microfiber, and nylon.

- Knife Blade – This is the other blade that comes in the box with the Cricut Maker. It can cut very thick materials. It gets through the same materials as the other blades, as well as tooling leather, balsa wood, basswood, heavy chipboard, and matboard.

32.   What is the scoring wheel?

A scoring wheel is a tool for the Cricut Maker, as it uses the Adaptive Tool System. It creates fold lines in thicker materials. The Scoring Stylus also makes fold lines, but the Scoring Wheel is more powerful and can score thicker materials.

33.   How small can the rotary blade cut?

Cricut recommends keeping designs above ¾". Any smaller than that, the blade might gouge into your mat as it turns, damaging the mat and dulling the blade.

34.   Where do I buy Cricut Blades?

You can buy blades where Cricut brand products are sold, including craft stores, superstores, Cricut's website, and other online stores.

Conclusion

This guide has brought you a whole new light of your creativity, knowing no boundaries with this wonderful machine. I hope we have helped you master the Cricut Design Space. It is a great little machine that can do so many different operations and allows you to make designs for inside and outside your home, to keep, to sell, and to give as gifts.

Cricut may seem complicated at first, but there is a lot you can do with this machine – and a lot that you can get out of it. If you feel confused by Cricut, then take your time, get familiar with the buttons, and start having fun with it.

With Cricut, anything is possible. If you have been wondering what you can do with your machine, the simple answer is almost anything. For designers, for those who like to make precise cuts, and for those who like to print their own shirts, this is a wonderful option to consider. If you are thinking of getting a Cricut machine, you will see here that there is a lot that you can do with this unique tool, and endless creative possibilities.

The next step is simple – if you have a Cricut machine, get familiar with it. Learn more about it and see for yourself some of the fun things you can do with Cricut, and the cool basic projects you can try now.

It can help you make a lot of handmade things which not only save you money but your time as well blessing you with beautiful products that you can use for yourself as well as the gift to others. You can make handmade cards, design your t- shirt, create your ornaments, and design an envelope and many more.

If you have yet to purchase your first machine, I hope this helps your decision. We want you to enjoy Cricut Design Space and much as thousands of users around the world.

Keep the tips and tricks provided close by as a reference guide so you are not searching all over to find the answers to your questions.

Never stop doing research. Never stop trying new things. Never, ever stop being creative. The Cricut does not make you any less creative; it just makes the process easier so that you can focus your valuable time and efforts on more important things or personalizing the projects after making the cuts. It takes the tedious work out of your hands and makes everything fun, easy, and fast.

Nowadays everyone could use a little extra cash. Your first of many cricut projects will be to make an assortment of about 10 to 12 cards. Be creative, there are a ton of ideas you can think of. Included in this assortment you should have a couple of Birthday cards (make sure you make cards for women, men and also cards for children), make sure to include Thank You, Anniversary, Get Well and even a Sympathy card.

CRICUT PROJECT IDEAS FOR BEGINNERS:

Tips And Tricks To Craft Out Your Projects Thanks To A Complete Guide With Illustrations. A Book To Explore That Can Inspire Your Imagination And Creativity.

Introduction

We should not forget that the cool thing about Cricut is that projects are endless. You might decide to have your own wall lettering, or you might choose to make a nursery at home, and you would need to make that distinct wall painting with several letters. Instead of you to spend several hours cutting with blades and carving with knives or any other cutting device, you just need a Cricut machine. You do not even need to hire a muralist for your hand painting because you can do that yourself. In fact, people like these are happy that you are not exposed to this knowledge so that they can make some cash from you. The die cut machine produces those precise cuts which children and other professional needs. There are several die-cut stickers you can get from this machine. This machine also allows you to render wedding favors and party favors quickly by helping in the creating process of tags, bags, boxes, and several other party creations. These pieces can come in several forms like gift bags, banners, hats, etc. these and many more can fit the theme of any party because you are making them. As much as I would love to shy away from the scrapbook stuff I just cannot. Now, just picture your daughter or your son getting married and you present him/her with a scrapbook having pictures from the very first day they stepped into this planet to where they are now. Gifts like this sound odd, but they are invaluable because you are not giving out a utensil or a tool you are giving out those memories. Scrapbooks carry out a lot of memories and those feelings you cannot give through your regular gifts.

If you have a Cricut machine and you have not gotten these supplies I would advise that you get them as soon as possible. We are aware that these supplies are grouped into different categories. First is the paper category which includes; adhesive cardstock, cereal box, copy paper, flocked paper, cardboard paper, Notebook paper, flocked cardstock, foil embossed paper, Freezer Paper, Glitter Paper, Kraft paper, Kraft Board, metallic Paper, Metallic Poster board, Photographs, Photo Framing Mat, Poster Board, Rice Paper, Wax Paper, Solid core Cardstock, White Core Cardstock, Photo Framing mat, Watercolor Paper, Freezer Paper, Foil Poster Board, etc.

We should not forget that the Vinyl is another material which you need to make your work on the Cricut machine smooth. The Cricut machine can work on those delicate materials which can be used to make decals, stencils, graphics, and those beautiful signs too. You can cut through the following vinyl materials, chalkboard vinyl, dry erase vinyl, holographic vinyl, stencil vinyl, printable vinyl, Matte Vinyl, Adhesive Vinyl, Printable Vinyl, and Glossy Vinyl also. Furthermore, you may have so much experience in the fabric and Textile world, and you want to infuse the Cricut machine. Some of the materials or fabrics that you can work with are; canvas, denim, cotton fabric, linen, leather, flannel, burlap, duck cloth, felt, metallic leather, polyester, printable materials, silk, wool felt and many more others. If you have not got your Iron on Vinyl. Which is meant to be the heat transfer vinyl. You make use of this vinyl to decorate a T-shirt, tote bags and other kind of fabric items that you can think of like; Printable Iron On, Glitter Iron on, Glossy Iron On, Flocked Iron on, Holographic sparkle iron on, Metallic Iron on, Neon Iron on, Foil Iron on, etc.

We should not narrow our minds to the materials mentioned above because there are several other materials which the Cricut can cut through or even work on some of them include; adhesive wood, cork board, Balsa Wood, craft foam, aluminum sheets, corrugated paper, Embossable foil, Foil Acetate, Paint Chips, Plastic Packaging, Metallic Vellum, Printable Sticker Paper, Stencil material, Shrink Plastic, Wrapping Paper, Window Cling, Wood Veneer, Washi Tape, Birch Wood, Wrapping Paper, Wood Veneer, Plastic Packaging, Soda Can, Glitter Foam, Printable Magnet Sheets, etc. The Cricut maker can work on materials which are up to 2.4mm thick and other unique materials and distinctive fabrics like the; Jersey, Cashmere, Chiffon, Terry Cloth, Tweed, Velvet, Jute, Knits, Moleskin, Fleece, and several others.

This machine can be found anywhere and everywhere, so much paper artwork is done. What this suggests is that you can see these machines in schools, offices, craft shops, etc. you can make use of this Cricut machine for a school project, card stock projects as well as iron-on projects too. Making use of this machine to cut out window clings is not a bad idea at all. It is not limited to this because you also engage in projects that have to do with adhesive stencil and stencil vinyl also.

You would remove the stencil vinyl after it is dried. This would leave a distinct imprint. You can also make use of this machine to create lovely fashion accessories like several pieces of jewelry. The Cricut machine allows you to make use of the faux leather for exceptional designs. Recall that we talked about school projects. Preschoolers and their instructors can benefit from this machine. Furthermore, you can print out photos or images from your computer while making use of this machine, especially from the printable magnets to those sticker papers, customized gifts, bags, etc.

Defining objects requires you to use other similar purposes to drive home your point and to give the reader a clearer picture. The very possible way we can describe a Cricut machine is to say that it is a machine that has so much resemblance with the printer, but it is used majorly for cutting designed pieces. That is a straightforward and easy definition you do not need to bother yourself about that. Just picture a printer in your mind and think of a cutting device. Oh, no, you already have the Cricut machine with you, right? You would notice that it uses precise blades and several templates or rollers during cutting.

Against what people think. The machine is not meant for scrapbook keepers or makers alone. I still do not know why this idea has become so much rooted in the minds of people that we have grown to allow this thought to dominate our reactions and attitude towards any new innovation.

The world has been transformed with that machine as its products have been able to add those unique visual beauties to the simple

119

paperwork that we know. The Cricut machine has several models and versions some of them include Cricut Expression, Expression 2, Cricut Imagine, Cricut Gypsy, Cricut Cake Mini, Cricut Personal Cutter, Cricut Crafts Edition and Martha Stewart and the Cricut Explore air. The tool obviously fits into any type of craft you are working on. And there is also a die cut machine which gives you that extra-precise, sharp, and smart cutting. The process of cutting materials by hand during crafts has been reduced drastically, thanks to this beautiful machine. More also, you can perform multiple projects all at the same time due to the effectiveness of this device. It contains several cartridges which are always available to help you explore different forms and shapes of several designs. More also that move from one project to another has been made possible with the use of this Cricut machine.

Any material can be shaped into that design you want it to be. Furthermore, you can also create patterns which are already pre-installed in the software that comes with it. The design software tool becomes very much available with pre-loaded designs for instant use. I am sure you must have been able to purchase this machine from your local craft store on the online store. You are aware that the price was based on the kind of model you are using and I am sure that you've been able to narrow down your needs for you to be able to get your machine because anything which makes your work easier and faster is a significant investment and the Cricut machine is definitely one. Due to the efficiency of this machine, we now have it in several places we never thought it would be in years. We have them in offices and specific workshops. If you feel that the Cricut is a home-only tool, you are entirely wrong. This time-saving device allows your work to be very professional, and the beautiful thing about it is that we have no limits to what it can do. I am sure that you are reading this to gain more ideas and you hastily want to jump into making things and doing some stuff. Yes, that is cool; however, we need to understand some basics else we would be making serious mistakes, or the process would look very confusing.

Chapter 1

A Simple Birthday Card

There are over 50,000 predesigned images in Cricut Design Space library. Therefore, you have a lot of pictures to play with when designing your greeting cards. So, how do you use your Cricut machine to create beautiful and super exciting cards? Not to worry as I will take you through the step by step approach on how to do those fantastic greeting cards.

The materials for this project include Cricut machine, computer, cardboard papers, Cricut writing pens, glue, micro glaze, and a pair of scissors.

It is crucial that I mention what the micro glaze is and what it is used for. Micro glaze is a protective cream wax for coating of paper and art. It also adds a little shin to the paper's print out. It is, therefore, essential for this project.

1. First open a new project on your Design space.

2. Go to Insert images and type in cards. You will see hundreds of free images.

3. Click on Insert shapes and select Square.

4. Navigate to the edit panel, unlock the lock by clicking the Unlock button.

5.   Select your desired size of the card. For example, the average size of A2 paper is 8.5X5.5" or you can use 5X7". It is your choice finally.

6.   Hit the Enter button on your computer.

7.   You need a score line at the center of the square. So click on the inserted Images to select it and you get to see the score line. Click on it and position on the top middle of the square and drag it down to the bottom part of the square. If you are not sure that the score line is at the center of the square, then all you need is draw a box around the score line, click on Align button at the top of the Canvas and select Center. Make sure you attach the score line to the square. To attach it, select the square and the score line together and choose connect in the Layer's panel. In the Layer's Panel, the two shapes will be white in colour if they are not selected but if selected, the pigment turns blue.

8.   You can change the colour of the square to any colour of your choice or continue in the next step.

9.   Select shapes again, unlock it and drag it down to cover half of the square.

10.   At this point you can play around with colours and shapes on the square to find which one tickle your fancy.

11.   Select Text tool and type in your desired text, edit the text using fonts, size, weld, slice, and many more on your screen. Some brief definitions and uses of the Edit tool have been described

in Chapter One, so, take your time to study them or read them in the literatures.

12.   As I stated earlier, there are lots of predesigned cards in the Design Space which you can play with if you do not have time to start designing your own image. But there is a catch though; you cannot share the files if it has uploaded images on it. Try to alter any shared images if you must use it in your design.

13.   When done, click on Print, then click on patterns to send it to the mat.

14.   Insert your colour marker to the left compartment of the adaptive tool in the machine. To load your pen is super easy. All you need do is open the clamp of your accessory A, uncap the appropriate pen as shown on the Design Space, push the pen inside the fitting A, press it until you hear a clicking sound, finally clamp your accessory A and you are good to go.

15.   Place your paper to be cut on the mat and then load it into the machine. Press the Load/Unload button and press the flashing Cricut button to start the job.

16.   Repeat step 15 for all the layers you have designed. You will need at least three coats for the design because of the outer cover of the card.

17.   After printing and cutting your write up, remove from the mat, and apply a little micro glaze on the printed surface.

18.   Arrange the other layers, ink the edges where there is the need to, apply glue to the printed paper before attaching it to it position on the card and fold the score line properly. In fact, as the project continues from step 15, you are already getting the feeling of a super crafter, right? I understand that feeling too.

Chapter 2

Welcome to Our Happy Home" Sign

A beautiful "Welcome to Our Home Sign" can warm up any entry hall. Choose a beautiful piece of wood, paint it a light color, then use your Cricut to make an excellent sign to put on it. Use a chalk finish paint to paint your board and use a bit of sandpaper to make it a little rough to help the vinyl stick. You can customize the sign to say anything you want, but for this exercise, we are going to use "Welcome to Our Happy Home."

Project Tools, Materials, and Accessories:

- A square wooden board the size you want your sign to be

- Baby blue paint with a matte or chalk finish — paint the wood before making the sign

- Permanent outdoor vinyl — black

- Green StandardGrip cutting mat

- Cricut Fine-Point Blade

- Pair of scissors for cutting the material to size

- Weeder tool

- Spatula

- Brayer for smoothing out the material

Directions:

1. Take the measurement of your board the width and length.

2. In Design Space, select 'Shapes' from the left-hand menu and choose a square.

3. Resize the square by typing in the dimensions of your board.

4. You will need to zoom the shape in to be able to see it on the screen.

5. You can have the background of the form in any color. If your text is going to be white, you may want to consider making the box black.

6. Next, you will need to choose a font for the writing on your sign.

7. Click on the 'Text' option on the right-hand side menu bar.

8. Type "Welcome to Our Happy Home."

9. Position the text onto the box frame on the screen mimicking where you are going to position the writing on your signboard.

10. For this project, choose Aaron Script single-layer cutting font. It is a lovely curly font for a sign.

11. Choose the color you want the writing for your sign to be. For the sake of this exercise, we are going to make the font black.

12. . Drag the corner of the text box to size the font to how big you want to make it. It must fit comfortably on your signboard.

13. Remove your template box as you no longer need it and it is not going to be cut.

14. Now is also an excellent time to save your project and give it a name you will recognize for future similar projects.

15. Make sure you have the correct size cutting board.

16. Cut the vinyl to the size you need. If you have made your fonts to fit completely across your sign, make sure the piece is big enough to fit your signboard.

17. Place the vinyl on the Cricut cutting mat. Here is a tip for you: If your rug is losing its stickiness, you need a bit of tape to anchor it firmly to the mat.

18. In Design Space, click 'Make It' in the top right-hand corner of the screen.

19. Set the material to vinyl.

20. You do not need a pen or accessory in the first holder, but you will need to use the fine-point blade in the second holder.

21. Load the cutting board with the vinyl and press the 'Load\Unload' button.

22. When the light flashes, the Cricut is loaded and ready to press 'Go.'

23. Gently peel back the vinyl. You may need to use the spatula to help peel the back vinyl off.

24. Use the weeder tool to hook away any vinyl from the middle of the words, for instance, the V-indent on top of the M. Try not to let any vinyl you have hooked fall back down as it may land crookedly and mess up your letter.

25. Once you have cleaned the vinyl from the words, use the transfer tape and ease it over the letters. Smooth it over the letters as best you can as you pull the back sheet of the transfer tape off. Try not to get bubbles in the tape by using the brayer to smooth the tape out.

26. Once you have the transfer tape on the letters, position it where you want to lay it out on your signboard.

27. If you feel you need guidelines, draw them out with a pencil.

28. Gently peel the white side of the transfer tape from the writing. Then position the top part of the sign where you want to start it on your signboard. Smooth out the rest of the flag.

29. Once the letters are positioned and stuck down with the top part of the transfer tape, give them a rub to ensure they are stuck down.

30. Gently pull the top of the transfer tape off the wording and your sign is ready.

Chapter 3

Personalized Paper Bookmark

Supplies needed are as follows:

- Cricut machine

- Printable sticker paper

- Inkjet printer

Instructions

1.   Log in to the Cricut design spaces.

2.   Start a new project and click on the Images at the screen's left side. Select the image(s) you want.

3.   Click on the Text icon and input your text.

4.   Select the font of your desire from the available font package.

5.   Highlight the documents and change the color by using the available colors on the color tray.

6.   Click on the Print option to change the file from a cut file to a print file.

7.   Click on the Ungroup icon to adjust the spacing of the text.

8.   After adjusting the spacing, highlight all and use the Group icon to make them one whole piece again.

9.   Click on the Shape icon and insert a shape.

10.   Change the shape's color using the color tray.

11Highlight the text and use the Align drop-down box.

12.   Make use of the Move to Front icon to move the text to front.

13.   Highlight the design and click on Group.

14.   Highlight the whole image and use the Flatten button to solidify the design as one whole piece.

15.   Resize the design to the appropriate size you need. You realize this by clicking on the model then dragging the right side of the box to the extent you desire.

16.   Click Save at the top left to save your project. Save it to be a Print and Cut image, after which you click the Make It button at the right hand of the screen.

17.   Examine the end result and click Continue if it is what you expected. This will lead you to print the design onto the paper.

18.   Adjust the dial on the Cricut machine to the required settings.

19.   Place the sticker paper on the cutting mat.

20.   Load the cutting mat into the machine and push it against the rollers.

21.   Press the Load/Unload button and then the Go button to cut the sticker.

22Your planning sticker is ready.

Chapter 4

Wedding Invitations

Materials needed – "Cricut" cutting machine, cutting mat, and cardstock or your choice of decorative paper/crepe paper/fabric, home printer (if not using "Cricut Maker").

Step 1

Use your "Cricut ID" to log in to the "Design Space" application. Then click on the "New Project" button on the top right corner of the screen to start a new project and view a blank canvas.

Step 2

A beginner-friendly way to create wedding invitations is a customization of an already existing project form the "Design Space" library that aligns with your own ideas. Click on the "Projects" icon on the "Design Panel" then select "Cards" from the "All Categories" drop-down. Enter the keywords "wedding invite" in the search bar.

Step 3

You can click on the project to preview its description and requirements. Once you have found the plan you want to use, click "Customize" at the bottom of the screen, so you can edit the invite and add the required text to it.

Step 4

The design will be loaded on to the canvas. Click on the "Text" button and type in the details for your invite. You will be able to modify the font, color as well as the alignment of the text from the "Edit Text Bar" on top of the screen. You can even adjust the size of the entire design as needed. (An invitation card can be anywhere from 6 to 9 inches wide)

Note – Most cards will require you to change the "Fill" to "Print" on the top of the screen so you can first print then cut the invitation.

Step 5

Select the entire design and click on the "Group" icon on the top right of the screen under "Layers Panel." Then click on the "Save" button to enter a name for your project and click "Save" again.

Step 6

Your design can now be printed then cut. Simply click on the "Make It" button on the top right corner of the screen to view the required mats and material. Then use your home printer to print the design on your chosen equipment (white cardstock or paper), or if using the "Cricut Maker," then just follow the prompts on the "Design Space" application.

Tip – Calibrate your machine first for the "Print then Cut" project by clicking on the hamburger icon next to the "Canvas" on the top left of the screen and follow the prompts on the screen, as shown in the picture below.

Step 7

Load the material with printed design to your "Cricut" cutting machine and click "Continue" at the bottom right corner of the screen to start reducing your design.

Note – If images and fonts used for your design are not free and available for purchase only, then the "Continue" button will not appear, and instead, a "Purchase" button will be visible. Once you have paid for the image or font, the "Continue" button will be available to you.

Step 8

Once your "Cricut" device has been connected to your computer, set the cut setting to "cardstock." Then place the printed cardstock on top of the cutting mat and load into the "Cricut" device by pushing against the rollers. The "Load/Unload" button would already be flashing, so just press that button first, followed by the flashing "Go" button. Viola! You have your wedding invitations already to be put in an envelope and on their way to all your wedding guests.

Chapter 5

Easy Diy Throw Pillow

Level- Easy

CREDIT- THECRAFTEDSPARROW.COM Whenever I am thinking of changing my décor; I always begin with switching out a throw pillow. I usually freshen up the look of my room with those little pillows that make vast differences. From all the projects that we have been doing, you must have noticed that starting something from scratch can be real time consuming. I love a new quick DIY design, which is why I make use of the Cricut Iron-on designs. You are going to be taught how to do so.

SUPPLIES NEEDED

-       Cricut Iron-On Designs (personal or downloaded to later upload on your design space)

-       The Cricut Easy press

-       The Cricut Easy press Mat

-       Ikea Pillow Cover or any beautiful already made pillow cover

-       Pillow inserts

- Some Yarn Tassels or Some Extra-Large Pom-Poms

STEP 1

You begin by making sure your pillow is covered with smooth pillow edges. You get your pillow cover ready by making it smooth. While making use of these, you should think of your personal design or wordings. I chose Good Vibes Only here. Before ironing the design, you must set the EasyPress to that correct temperature for your material. I had a pillow cover cotton, so I placed it at 3400 With that time setting a record of 30 seconds. You might decide to reduce and increase the level because they would be divided into several heat settings which are required for each surface.

STEP 2

You should make sure that the design on the pillow cover is placed strategically at the center. You use your Cricut Easy press to hover around and hold it firmly in place for some 30 seconds. Do not forget to use the timer. Once the timer beeps, you know it is time to move to the next fragment of the design and do not forget to do the same.

STEP 3

The Cricut EasyPress is very convenient and very easy to use. I should tell you that you can use the EasyPress for everyday ironing also. Are you aware? The EasyPress is excellent stuff because it covers an extensive surface area more than your regular iron. You are to reveal the iron-on design by doing a cold peel. What this means is that you should let cool off completely before removing that protective transparent sheet that is over it.

STEP 4

After this, you can decide to embellish your pillow. This is entirely up to you. In this project, I was working with a premade pillow cover, so I decided to go with something simple and straightforward. I went with the DIY yarn tassel for the project. You might decide to do pom-poms, pom-pom trim, or you might just leave it the way it is. That is your decision, but I am sure you would want to make some designs.

For the tassel, you would wrap that your yarn around that piece of cardboard. For this project, I wrapped mine over and over again like a hundred times because I wanted them to be big and chunky. Next was that I trimmed them with those sewing shears.

STEP 5

To add those tassels to the strategic corners, you would unstitch a very tiny spot on each side of the pillow cover with your seam ripper. Then you would insert the shot tassel string making use of some hot glue to seal it shut and secure it. Then you can also stitch them into that place that you want. I made use of a quick and easy way with the hot glue.

Lastly, you add your pillow to that corner of the room. Simple!

Chapter 6

Stenciled Welcome Mat and Unicorn Wine Glass

MATERIALS NEEDED:

Cricut Machine

Scrap cardstock (The color does not matter)

Coir mat (18" x 30")

Outdoor acrylic paint

Vinyl stencil

Transfer tape

Flat round paintbrush

Cutting mat (12" x 24")

Photo credit- youtube.com

STEPS:

• Create your design in Cricut Design Space. You can also download an SVG design of your choice and import it into Cricut Design Space. Make sure that your plan is the right size; resize it to ensure that this is so.

- Next, you are to cut the stencil. You do this by clicking "Make it" in Cricut Design Space when you are done with the design. After this, you select "Cardstock" as the material. Then, you press the "Cut" button on the Cricut machine.

- When this is done, remove the stencil from the device and weed.

- Next, on the reverse side of the stencil, apply spray glue. After this, attach the stencil to the doormat, exactly where you want your design to be; then, pick up the letter bits left on the cutting mat and glue them to their places in the stencil on the doormat.

- The next step is to mask the parts of the doormat which you do not want to paint on. You can do this using painters' plastic.

- Now, it is time to spray-paint your stencil on the doormat. Keeping the paint can about 5 inches away from the doormat, spray up and down, keeping the can point straight through the stencil. If it is at an angle, the paint will get under the stencil and ruin your design. Spray the entire stencil 2-3 times to make sure that you do not miss any part and that the paint is even.

- You are just about done! Now, remove the masking plastic and the stencil and leave the doormat for about one hour to get dry.

Unicorn Wine Glass

Who does not love unicorns? Who does not enjoy wine? Bring them together with these glittery wine glasses! The outdoor vinyl will hold up to use and washing, and the Mod Podge will keep the glitter in place for years to come. Customize it even more with your own quote. You could use a different magical creature as well—mermaids go fabulous with glitter too! Customize this to suit your tastes or to create gifts for your friends and family. Consider using these for a party and letting the guests take them home as favors!

Supplies Needed

Stemless wine glasses

Outdoor vinyl in the color of your choice

Vinyl transfer tape

Cutting mat

Weeding tool or pick

Extra fine glitter in the color of your choice

Mod Podge

Instructions

Open Cricut Design Space and create a new project.

Select the "Text" button in the Design Panel.

Type "It's not drinking alone if my unicorn is here."

Using the dropdown box, select your favorite font.

Adjust the positioning of the letters, rotating some to give a whimsical look.

Select the "Image" button on the Design Panel and search for "unicorn."

Select your favorite unicorn and click "Insert," then arrange your design how you want it on the glass.

Place your vinyl on the cutting mat, making sure it is smooth and making full contact.

Send the design to your Cricut.

Use a weeding tool or pick to remove the excess vinyl from the design. Use the Cricut Bright Pad to help if you have one. Apply transfer tape to the design, pressing firmly, and making sure there are no bubbles.

Remove the paper backing and apply the words to the glass where you would like them. Leave at least a couple of inches at the bottom for the glitter.

Smooth down the design and carefully remove the transfer tape.

Coat the bottom of the glass in Mod Podge, wherever you would like glitter to be. Give the area a wavy edge.

Sprinkle glitter over the Mod Podge, working quickly before it dries.

Add another layer of Mod Podge and glitter and set it aside to dry.

Cover the glitter in a thick coat of Mod Podge.

Allow the glass to cure for at least 48 hours.

Enjoy drinking from your unicorn wine glass!

Chapter 7

Custom Coasters and Halloween T-Shirt

Personalize your home with this sweet little project or give a gift as for a housewarming party or holiday. You can do abstract designs and words like the example or make it more personal with photos and images if you want.

You will need:

- Cork for cutting on your Cricut

- Adhesive Vinyl

- Adhesive Felt or felt tabs

- Transfer Tape

Step 1

In Design Space, decide what size and shape of a coaster you want to create. Traditional coasters are often circular or square, but like the example shows, you do not need to be bound to those shapes for your coasters. Make sure you also have the quantity you plan to make in mind.

Step 2

When you have your design laid out, send the bottom shapes to cut out of the cork material.

Step 3

Once your cork is cut, use the coaster shapes in Design Space to now design the images, words, or other details to your coasters. You can make each coaster the same design, or you can use a theme and create custom messages for each one. It can be helpful to add dates, monograms, and photographs instead of shapes and sayings. Make sure whatever you decide will fit on the coasters you just cut out.

Once you have these laid out, send your file to cut from the colored vinyl you have chosen. Weed out any unnecessary parts and then use transfer tape to move your vinyl from its backing to your project. Smooth out the plastic with your scraper tool before removing the tape.

Step 4

Using an Exacto knife, lay your coasters on top of the adhesive felt and cut around the shape. Peel off the backing and apply the felt to the underside of the coaster. If you are using felt tabs instead, make sure there is a tab at least at every corner or few inches on the bottom of your coaster. If you want a raise coaster, you could even cut designs from the felt and add it over the vinyl on top!

It is not necessary to add the felt pieces on the bottom of the cork, but it does add a more professional touch to your project. It also adds extra protection for your furniture, where you will be using the coasters.

Halloween T-Shirt

MATERIALS NEEDED:

T-shirt Blanks

Glam Halloween SVG Files

Cardstock

Transfer Sheets (Black and Pink)

Butcher Paper (comes with Infusible Ink rolls)

LightGrip Mat

EasyPress (12" x 10" size recommended)

EasyPress Mat

Lint Roller

STEPS:

- Import the SVG files into Cricut Design Space and arrange them as you want them on the T-shirt.
- Change the sizes of the designs to get them to fit on the T-shirt.
- Using the slice tool, slice the pink band away from the hat's bowler part (the most significant piece). Make a copy of this band, and then slice it from the lower part of the

hat. With these done, you will have three pieces that fit together.

- You can change the designs' colors as you would like them. When you are done with the preparation, click "Make It".

- Ensure that you invert your image using the "Mirror" toggle. This is even more important if there is text on your design, as infusible ink designs should be done in inverse. This is because the part with the ink is to go right on the destination material.

- Click on "Continue"

- For the material. Select Infusible ink. After this, cut the design out using your Cricut Machine.

- With the designs cut out, weed the transfer sheet.

- Cut around the designs such that the transfer tape does not cover any part of the infusible ink sheet. Make sure that this is done well as any part of the infusible ink that is not in contact with the fabric will not be transferred.

- Preheat your EasyPress to 385 degrees and set your EasyPress mat.

- Prepare your T-shirt by placing it on the EasyPress mat, then using a lint roller to remove any lint from the front.

- Insert the Cardstock in the t-shirt, between the front and back, just where the design will be. This will protect the other side of the T-shirt from having the Infusible Ink on it.

- If necessary, use the lint roller on the T-shirt again, after which you should heat your shirt with the EasyPress. Do this at 385 degrees for 15 seconds.

- Turn the part where the design faces on the T-shirt. Place the butcher paper on the map, ensuring, again, that the backing does not overlap the design.

- Place the EasyPress over the design and hold it in place for 40 seconds. Do not move the EasyPress around so that your plan does not end up looking smudged.

- Remove the EasyPress from the shirt and remove the transfer sheet.

- To layer colors, ensure that your cutting around the transfer sheet is done as close as possible, then repeat the previous three steps for each color. This will prevent the transfer sheet from removing part of the color on the previously transferred design.

Chapter 8

Letterboard DIY Builder Cricut Knife

Had you used the knife blade, Cricut Maker? You have to go for it, I think! The knife blade is a pioneering device maker for Cricut, which makes completely impossible tasks otherwise! The Cricut creator knife is a good board with letters in this style.

Materials needed:

Cricut-maker (sorry, no other cutter can do this)

The Cricut-maker is different from any other cutter. It is reliable, ultimately, reduce, and extremely versatile! It is powerful!

Cricut blade knife (able to cut materials as thick as 2.4 mm) Cricut agglomerate

12x18 Purple Cricut Craft Foam Mat 12X24

Pine blue painters' tape 12x12 Board

1x2 boards cut to 12 "hot glue School

System Tuning Tools Cricut enables the blade, turning blade, scoring wheel to use ... and who knows what is coming! Let us talk about a second blade knife.

The materials that the knife blade is rated cutting are:

Cricut agglomerate, 2 mm matboard, two- or four-layers Craft foams up to 3 mm Balsa wood, up to 3/32 "linden to 1/16"

Leather ball, up to 7 ounces.

If you have not used the knife blade before doing so, you must first calibrate the Blad. Go to your dresser CDS ...

Click calibration and then the knife blade. Now do as the instructions say.

Put the knife blade, use the green baize, and place it on the machine with a lightweight piece of paper. Then go ahead. The knife blade makes multiple small cuts and asks you what are the most compatible. Respond to instructions and is ... ready to cut.

Remember to slide the edges of the star to the right of the bar using the knife blade. It prevents the material from being cut grooving and grooving. •

Now adhere to the foam mat purple of his art and see the edges with painter's upholstery. Install the Maker Cricut sheet. Replace the mat later.

I designed the project design Cricut space, which will provide a large number of letters. Craft Foam set things ... 2 passes to be performed.

Try and see if the cut has gone through the material before removing the pad. A pass more, I had to do. Draw all letters and then removes the pad.

These fun letters give so many choices!

Cut support pieces agglomerate Cricut with the Creator. Cricut agglomerate is different from other cardboard boxes and therefore is designed for blade knife and maker.

Write down the agglomerate into a carpet of purple, the same idea as before.

Place one letter on each table instead. Play them all in one seat or just select the phrase you like, and then mount it.

Use hot glue to add foam letters handmade his agglomerate.

You are carrying Letterboard together now. It is so simple! If you have no power tool to cut the package.

You have to do everything in one seat and some 2x3

Measure the table beside pine and mark four and eight. Back to the other side of the marking process.

Run-on one side of a strip of 1x2, a squiggle school, or wood glue.

Below joints immediately above labels, plus the latest in the bottom right.

Chipboard letters rest on the wall below.

The agglomerate is heavy enough to hold everything perfectly in place! So really- I think you should go for this Cricut knife blade creator if you have not used it!

Chapter 9

Thanksgiving Floral Wreath

C reate a simple, festive wreath to adorn your door this holiday season. Pick up cardstock in a variety of analogous colors or patterns, with one "pop" of color to stand out, like the teal color in the image above, and a variety of greens for the leaves.

You will also need a foam wreath form, in any size you choose, and a hot glue gun. A small amount of matching fabric is nice to have, but not necessary if you are in a bind. For added details, have a few felt balls, beads, or small buttons on hand that match your project as well.

Step 1

This wreath is a makeup of three different flowers: long petal, petal, and fold over. You will want to make a variety of these is different sizes and colors. Follow the instructions to make each type of flower:

- Long petal flower: Cut out the pattern and add a dot of glue at the beginning. Roll the pattern until it is completely together, and seal with another dot of glue. Smaller flowers tend to have only one later, while larger flowers have 3 or more. Beginning at the base of the flower, pull the petals down to shape them into a flower. At the end, pinch and shape the edge upwards.

- Petal flower: Smaller flowers need four larger petals and about six smaller ones. For larger flowers, you will want to scale up. For example, a medium petal flower would have six large petals and eight smaller petals. Pinch the base of the petals to make a point along the backside. Press the point down to flatten a bit with your finger. Take a small felt ball, button or bead and add a drop of glue to the pressed inside of the small petal. Press the small petal to the underside of the ball. Continue layering all the small petals around the ball, and then add the larger petals. Shape the top of the petals to create a flower appearance.

- Fold over flowers: Cut out the pattern and fold the design in half lengthwise. Place a line of glue along the edge and seal together. Add a dot of glue at the beginning of the pattern and begin to roll until the end. Seal with another dot of glue. Use your fingers to fluff and shape the petals.

Step 2

Cut out different leaf shapes from the green paper. Pinch the ends of the leaves to give them volume and a leaf shape.

Step 3

If you are using fabric, wrap the wreath with fabric, securing it to the form with glue. If you are not using fabric, or do not want it to show, make sure you have enough flowers to cover the entire wreath.

Step 4

Attach the flowers to the wreath using hot glue. Alternate the size and colors to space them evenly around the wreath. When you have attached all your flowers, glue the leaves to the wreath, filling in any open spots. Hang your wreath on your door or place it on your table as part of your centerpiece.

Chapter 10

Hand Lettered Cake Topper and

Window Stickers

D o you know with your Cricut machine you can add a different touch of creativity to that anniversary cake using a cake topper? It is super simple and also an easy DIY project for you to try using the step by step approach given below.

Another good thing about this project is that it requires a little budget, that is, if you already have your Cricut machine. The materials used for this project are also readily available.

The materials for this project include the Cricut Maker machine, a computer, Cricut spatula, light weight chip board and cake stick.

1.   Open a new project in your Cricut Design Space.

2.   Click on Text tool and type in your desired text.

3.   Change the text to your favorite font.

4.   Ungroup the letters and arrange them to be slightly overlapping as shown below. Do these, word by word, in case you have more than one word.

5.   Weld the word together separately.

6.   What if you have the letter "i" in your expression, how do you connect the floating dot? It is very simple. All you need to do is

1.   Go to shapes and select cycle.

2.   Resize the size of the cycle to be slightly bigger than the floating dot.

3.   Move the cycle over the floating dot.

4.   Select the whole word where the letter "i" is contained and then select slice. The essence of this is to separate the floating dot from the letter "I".

5.   Move the cycle back to join the letter "i" without the floating dot and weld it together.

7.   When you have done this for all the letters "I", join the words together by touching each other in as many places as possible. This will make the cake topper to be as stable as possible.

8.   Weld them all together.

9.   Resize it to taste by increasing or decreasing the dimensions.

10.   Now is time to make it.

11.   Send it to the mat.

12.   Set the dial to customs and select light weight chip board.

13.   Place your lightweight chip board on the mat and load it into the machine by pressing Load/Unload button.

14.   Press the flashing Cricut button.

15.   Use Cricut spatula to remove the cake topper from the mat when the job is done and after unloading the mat from the machine. You remember how to unload, right? Yes, you do.

16.   Remove the unwanted and extra chip board from your design.

17.   Finally attach your cake stick to middle of your design with the aid of glue. If you have a long expression, use two or more sticks depending on the size of your cake.

Window Stickers

Supplies needed are as follows:

- Cricut machine

- Printable sticker paper

- Inkjet printer Instructions

1.   Log in to the Cricut design space.

2.   Start a new project.

3.   Click on the Text icon and input your inspirational text.

4.   Select the font of your desire from the available font package.

5.   available colors on the color tray.

6. Click on the Print option to change the file to a print file from a cut file.

7. Click on the Ungroup icon to adjust the spacing of the text.

8. After adjusting the spaces, highlight all and use the Group icon to make them one whole piece again.

9. Click on the Shape icon and insert a shape.

10. If it is a rectangle you need, insert a square, unlock the shape, and drag it to a rectangle.

11. Change the shape's color using the color tray.

12. Highlight the text and use the Align drop-down box.

13. Make use of the Move to Front icon to move the text to front.

14. Highlight the design and click on Group.

15. Duplicate the label as much as the screen allows.

16. Highlight the whole design and use the Flatten icon to keep it together during printing.

17. Highlight the design and right-click, then select Attach.

18. Click on the Go button and print the design on the printable sticker paper.

Adjust the dial on the Cricut machine to the custom sticker paper settings.

20. Place the sticker paper on the cutting mat.

21. Load the cutting mat into the machine and push it against the rollers.

22. Press the Load/Unload button, and then make use of the Go button to cut the stickers.

23. Your inspirational quotes sticker is ready to be used.

Chapter 11

Motivational Water Bottle and Keep Your Distance Car Window Stickers

E veryone needs a motivational boost to keep their workouts going. Turn a boring water bottle into your personal cheerleader! Choose the type of water bottle that you like the best, whether it is a plastic, glass, or metal one. This could also work on a reusable tumbler if you prefer to have a straw. The glitter vinyl will give a fun accent to your necessary hydration, but you can change it to a regular color if you want to be a bit less flashy. Use one of the suggested quotes or one of your own. The important thing is that it motivates you to keep moving!

Supplies Needed

Sturdy water bottle of your choice

Glitter vinyl

Vinyl transfer tape

Light grip cutting mat

Weeding tool or pick

Instructions

Open Cricut Design Space and create a new project.

Measure the space on your water bottle where you want the text and create a box that size.

Select the "Text" button in the lower left-hand corner.

Choose your favorite font and type the motivational quote you like best.

I sweat glitter

Sweat is magic

I do not sweat, I sparkle

Place your vinyl on the cutting mat.

Send the design to your Cricut.

Use a weeding tool or pick to remove the excess vinyl from the text.

Apply transfer tape to the quote.

Remove the paper backing from the tape.

Place the quote where you want it on the water bottle.

Rub the tape to transfer the vinyl to the bottle, making sure there are no bubbles. Carefully peel the tape away.

Bring your new water bottle to the gym for motivation and hydration!

Keep Your Distance Car Window Stickers

If you have ever wanted a car window decal sticker but cannot find one to suit your needs, you can make your own with the Cricut. There are so many fun things you can do with car window decals. Create fun sayings for the window, pictures of your favorite sport, different animals, and so on. If you are looking to sell your craft car window decals, they still have a large following in the market.

Project Tools, Materials, and Accessories:

- Outdoor glossy vinyl (clear or white)

- Green StandardGrip mat

- Cricut measuring tape

- Inkjet printer

- Transfer tape

- Rubbing alcohol

- Cricut Fine-Point Blade

- Weeding tool

- Spatula

- Brayer or scraping tool

- Pair of scissors for cutting the material to size

Directions:

1. Measure how big you are going to want the decal to be.

2. Open a new Design Space project.

3.   Select 'Images' from the left-hand menu.

4.   Type in "bear" in the search bar and choose the black bear (Image #MF7274E7).

5.   Position it on the screen and scale it to the desired size.

6.   Change the color of the bear to brown.

7.   Select 'Text' from the left-hand menu and reset the font to Bernard MT Condensed. It is a nice clear font with a bit of character.

8.   Type "Momma Bear on Board" on the one line.

9.   Hit enter and type "Keep Your Distance" on the next line.

10. Center the text and change the color to white.

11. Unlock the text and scale it to size, then position it in the center of the bear.

12. Make sure none of the letters hang over the side of the bear image.

13. Select both the bear image and text, then click 'Flatten' from the bottom right-hand menu. You can also right-click and choose 'Flatten.'

14. Save the project.

15. Click on 'Make it.'

16.   Make sure the image is aligned correctly on the page and everything is the way you want it to be.

17.   Click 'Continue.'

18.   Load your outdoor glossy vinyl sheet into your Inkjet printer. When you are ready, click 'Send to Printer.'

19.   Press 'Print' if you are happy with the print setup.

20.   Once the printer has finished printing the decal, unload the vinyl sheet from the Inkjet printer.

21.   Stick the printed decal onto the cutting mat.

22.   Go back to your project in Design Space and choose the correct material.

23.   Load the cutting mat into the Cricut, and when it is ready, press 'Go.'

24.   When it is done, use the spatula, if necessary, to pull off the backing sheet of the vinyl.

25.   Use the weeding tool to weed off any pieces that should not be there.

26.   Cut some transfer paper to the size of the decal.

27.   Place it over the decal. It is easier to work with it if it is stuck to the cutting mat.

28.   Use the brayer or scraping tool to smooth the transfer tape over the image and get all the bubbles out.

29.   Pull it off the cutting mat.

30.   Take the rubbing alcohol and clean the portion of the car window that you want to place the decal on.

31.   Gently pull the back of the vinyl off and position the decal on the cleaned window.

32.   Once it is on the window, use the brayer or scraping tool to smooth it out and ensure it is properly stuck down.

33.   Gently pull off the transfer tape and your decal are on your window.

Chapter 12

Baby Blanket and Gift Tags

This can be a great keepsake for the future, a useful daily item or even a unique and special gift. In fact, it does not have to be just for your baby. You can make one of these blankets for virtually any occasion.

You will need:

- Cricut machine

- Iron

- Iron-on fabric

- Standard cotton fabric or plain blanket – any color

Step 1

Go into the Design Space app and select the numbers or test you wish to add to your blanket. You will need to remove any negative spaces and reverse the letters and numbers. This is so that when they are stuck to your blanket they can be read properly.

You can choose a date of birth, a short phrase or even a picture. There is practically no limit to how many shapes you can create as long as they will fit on the blanket.

Step 2

Now you need to use your cricut machine to print and cut each letter and number onto your iron-on fabric. These should be ready to use as soon as they are printed.

You can then place them on your blanket and iron them into position.

The key here is to have a flat surface and then place a folded towel onto it. The blanket can go on top. This will allow your fabric to have a little flex which will ensure the edge of the images is stuck properly.

When ironing on the fabric you need to ensure the temperature is at least 305° Fahrenheit (150°C). Hold the iron over the image for approximately 30 seconds to ensure it sticks properly.

Gift Tags

This project is like making a greeting or thank you card outlined in the first chapter, but a more simplified process. It can pretty much be any design you can think of, but it does need to be a flat image.

You will need:

- Cardstock

- Selection of Cricut pens, if desired

Step 1

Open Design Space and import the images you want to use on your gift tags. This could include the shape of the tags, words, and colors of the tags.

Step 2

Once you lay out your gift tag designs, add a small circle to the top to be cut out. This is where you will pass string or ribbon through the tag. Once this last feature is added, send the file to cut by clicking on "Make It."

If you are interested in multi-dimensional tags, create layers with additional text or images that will be attached or strung together. Cricut will alert you when you need to add new paper to a cutting mat and how it should be relatively easy to assemble.

Step 3

Once the file is cut, remove from your cutting mat, and assemble your pieces. If there are any small pieces that are still stuck to your designs, like the small circle for your string or ribbon, use your weeding tool to remove the unwanted pieces. This is usually best done while still on the mat.

To add more decoration to your tags, consider adding a bit of glitter to the tags or extra little pieces, such as a small tree, star, or snowflake cut out.

Chapter 13

Hologram Party Box Tumblers and Party Decor Medallions

Instead of party goody boxes, why not try hologram personalized party tumblers stuffed with the goodies? The kids get their party treats inside an awesome tumbler to take home for later use.

Project Tools, Materials, and Accessories:

- Hologram stick-on vinyl

- Clear tumblers

- Green StandardGrip mat

- Cricut Fine-Point Blade

- Weeding tool

- Scraping tool or brayer tool

- Pair of scissors for cutting the material to size

Directions:

1. Open a new project in Design Space.

2. Select 'Square' from the 'Shapes' menu on the left-hand side menu.

3. Change the background color to grey.

4. Unlock the shape and change it to the width and height of the tumbler. The hologram will run from about 1" below the lip of the tumbler to 1" above the base.

5. To accurately measure the width of the hologram paper, wrap it around the tumbler and cut it.

6. Lay it flat on the cutting mat to get the hologram paper's dimensions.

7. Select 'Text' from the menu on the left-hand side.

8. Type in the person's name that the tumbler is for.

9. Select a nice chunky font that will work for the cutout.

10. Position the font onto the middle of the square on the screen.

11. Stretch it to fit across the square.

12.   Select both the square and the text.

13.   Right-click and choose 'Slice.'

14.   Select the first layer of the name text, move it off to one side, then delete it.

15.   Select the second layer of the name text, move it off to one side, then delete it.

16.   If you like, you can add an image and repeat steps 13 to 16 for the shape or image.

17.   When the hologram image is ready, select 'Make it.'

18.   Make sure the fine-point blade is loaded.

19.   Make sure the hologram vinyl is correctly stuck to the cutting mat.

20.   Select the correct material and press 'Go' once the Cricut is ready to cut.

21.   Once it has cut, leave the vinyl on the cutting board, and weed out the middle of the image and text.

22.   Place the transfer sheet over the vinyl and use the scraper or brayer tool to smooth it out.

23.   Remove the back sheet.

24.   Carefully place the hologram paper around the tumbler.

25.   Use the scraper to ensure it is on properly.

26.   Remove the transfer sheet.

Party Decor Medallions

You will need following things

- Records- 45 same size

- Poster board

- Scale

- Scissors

- Adhesive/Glue

- Vintage Milk Caps

- Twine

- Scrapbook

- Scallop Punch

In first step measurements are made and cutting is applied to paper. Fold many papers and cut them in once, paper with measurement of 6,5,4 inches in width for small, medium, and large medallions. By holding one end of paper fold it, repeat the folds backward and forth ward. All of the paper strips should be folded in a same way. Now attach all of the strips with the help of glue but in the way they become in the form of seamless strip. Squeeze the strips from the end and pull all of the strips to form it in a shape of a circle. By using glue take the record and attach it from lower portion of paper medallion. Now take 2.5 scallop and fix them with each other. Apply some glue to the center and fix the milk cap and center of the circle. On the back side of center top of medallion attach a twine piece; pass a string into it, now it is ready for hanging on the wall or in any other place.

Chapter 14

Napkin Holders and Magnetic Paper Flowers

Project thanks to Laura's Little Party

Make your next dinner party standout with personal and custom napkin holders. You can make them in any design you like to match your dinner party theme or season. You can also make it as simple as possible, with just a few images or words, or more complicated with multiple materials and pieces.

Choose a version based on your comfort and preference level. In addition, you can also decide how you want to attach your holders. For example, you can add small slits on the top on one end of the holder and one on the bottom of the other to slide into each other, or you can use a glue dot. You can even use a small strip of double-stick tape to enclose the holder. You could also add small holes on either side of the holder and lace ribbon or string through it.

You will need:

- Colored or glitter cardstock

- Vinyl, if preferred

- Your closure method of choice: glue dots, double-stick tape, etc.

Step 1

In Design Space, design the text or names that you want to appear on your napkin wraps. Make sure it is adjusted so the words will appear appropriately on your wrap width. This is also the time to develop a layer with the flourishing details, like the olive branch, and the shape of your napkin wrap. Also, think about images and different shapes you could include on your napkin holders.

Step 2

With your napkin wrap base designed, repeat your patterns and words on the number you need for your place settings. This is what will tell your Cricut to cut multiple pieces and allows you the opportunity to customize each one if you desire. If you are going to be closing the wraps with ribbon and need holes or want to slide the ends together with slits, make sure to add those in now.

Step 3

Once you have your designs laid out, send the file to cut. Weed out any small items you do not want in your design. Assemble your napkin wrap pieces and wrap your napkins or silverware for your big event! Make sure to attach them securely according to the method you have chosen.

Magnetic Paper Flowers

Adding a few bright flowers to your fridge can take your kitchen from average to extraordinary. It can help it go from a place you "have" to be to a place you "want" to be! You can create as many as you want, in any color or pattern that matches your décor. You can also come up with a variety of flowers to suit your mood or help you keep track of your family needs. They are also awesome gifts!

You will need:

- Cardstock in a variety of colors or patterns

- Hot glue gun

- Magnets

Step 1

Open Design Space and develop the shape of your petals. These look good as half circles or oval shapes. You can also create bumped petal shapes by stacking oval over one another. Repeat the petal shapes to make enough flower magnets that you want. A large flower typically has about 12 petals while a medium one has about eight. Medium petals are about two inches long while large petals are usually about three inches. Measure the size of your magnet base and develop a circular flower base. If you want to, you can add a small, ½ inch long slit at the end of every petal for easiest construction.

Step 2

Once you have your petals designed and duplicated, load the cardstock on your cutting mat and get it ready to cut. Send the file to cut. If you did not add the slit in Design Space, use a crafting knife or an Exacto knife to cut a slit at the bottom of each petal. Once all the petals have a cut, add a dot of glue and glue one side to the other making them into the petal shape. Do this to all the petals.

Step 3

Place your magnets down on the table and gather all the base circles and glue them to the tops of the magnets. Begin gluing the petals to the circle bases, starting on the outside and working your way in. Continue adding petals until it looks full. Large flowers will have about three or more layers, while medium may only have two. Keep playing with your petals until you have a shape and set up that looks best to you. Leave a small space in the center of the flower open.

Step 4

Go back to Design Space and create smaller petals. Make them slightly smaller than the first petals. These are designed to add to the center of your flowers, so adjust them according to what you want. If you are unsure, try a few different shapes to try them out. Add the slits to the petals again or wait until after they are cut to add the slits with an Exacto knife. When you are ready, send the file to cut. Create the petal shapes with a little bit of glue.

Step 5

Add glue to the interior of the flower design and begin adding the smaller petals to the inside of your flowers. Gently pinch the edges of your flowers for a more geometric appearance or gently curve them inside for something more natural. You can add as many petal layers as you like.

Chapter 15

Pet Name Collars

S ome Cricuts can cut softer metals such as aluminum, soft gold, brass, and so on. This allows for the making of dog tags, bracelets, earrings, plaques, and so on. For this project, you are going to use shapes to create dog bone name tags.

Project Tools, Materials, and Accessories:

- Cricut aluminum

- Purple Strong Grip mat

- Engraving tip (this fits on the scoring tool)

- Builder's tape

- Jewelry ring

Directions:

1. Open a new project in Design Space.

2. Select 'Square' from the 'Shapes' menu on the left-hand side menu.

3. Change the background color to grey.

4. Unlock the shape and change it to 8" wide and 8" long.

5. Select 'Square' from the 'Shapes' menu on the left-hand side.

6. Leave the background as it is.

7. Unlock the shape and change it to 4.056" wide and 2" long.

8. Select 'Circle' from the 'Shapes' menu on the left-hand side.

9. Leave the background as it is.

10. Unlock the shape and change it to 0.516" wide and 0.516" long.

11. Duplicate the circle.

12. Unlock the duplicate circle and change its dimensions to 0.316" wide and 0.316" long.

13. Position the smaller second circle over the first one directly in the middle.

14. Right-click and select 'Slice.'

15.   Select the circle, then remove and delete the two slices.

16.   Move the circle with the hole in it to sit on the top edge of the small square. Place it in the middle touching the edge of the square.

17.   Select the smaller square and the circle, right-click, and select 'Weld.'

18.   Select 'Heart' from the 'Shapes' menu on the left-hand side.

19.   Leave the background as it is.

20.   Unlock the shape and change it to 2.378" wide and 2.504" long.

21.   Rotate the heart until the rounded, curved side points to the right and the point of the heart points to the left of the screen.

22.   Position it on the right end of the smaller square about halfway to the middle of the heart.

23.   Duplicate the heart and move the duplicate heart to one side.

24.   Select the smaller square and heart, right-click, and select 'Weld.'

25.   Flip the duplicate heart horizontally so it mirrors the welded heart.

26.   Repeat steps 22 to 24.

27.   Move the dog bone onto the larger grey square.

28.   Select 'Text' from the menu on the left-hand side.

29.   Choose a font and type the dog's name on it. If you like, you can type a phone number, etc.

30.   Duplicate the dog bone tag as you can fit two of these tags onto one metal sheet.

31.   Change the text on the second dog bone shape.

32.   Remove and delete the larger grey square.

33.   Save project.

34.   Click 'Make it.'

35.   Put the engraver point on the rotary blade and place it into the Cricut machine.

36.   Move the star wheels to the right side of the feeding bar.

37.   Set the dial on the Cricut to custom.

38.   Stick the metal onto the Strong Grip mat.

39.   Stick the metal plate down with builder's tape around the edges so it is firmly attached.

40.   Load the mat into the Cricut.

41.   In Design Space, select the correct material and make sure the design lines up with the metal on the cutting mat.

42.   Press 'Continue' and 'Go' on the Cricut when it is ready to cut.

43.   Note that it does take quite a while to do the engraving.

44.   When the Cricut is finished cutting, remove the metal from the cutting mat.

45.   Pop the tags away from the excess metal and use the weeding tool as well as the tweezers to clean up the designs.

46.   Place a jewelry ring through the top little loops on top of the dog tags, and they are ready to attach to the dog's collar.

Chapter 16

Magnet Alphabet Fun with Iron-On Mosaic Squares

For this project, you will be using Cricut chipboard and Cricut holographic vinyl material. The letters will be magnetized so kids can spell out letters on a magnetic board.

Project Tools, Materials, and Accessories:

- Cricut chipboard

- Cricut holographic art deco permanent vinyl— this project uses red and green

- Purple Strong Grip mat

- Cricut Knife Blade

- Weeding tool

- Scraping tool or brayer tool

- Pair of scissors for cutting the material to size

- Hot glue gun

- 52 magnets 1" by 1" in size

- Builder's tape

Directions:

1. Open a new project in Design Space.

2. Select 'Square' from the 'Shapes' menu on the left-hand side.

3. Change the background color to grey.

4. Unlock the shape and change it to 11" wide and 11" long.

5. Zoom the screen to 50%.

6. Select 'Text' from the menu on the left-hand side.

7. Choose a nice font that is clear for children like 'Arial Black.'

8. Type out the alphabet in capital letters.

9. Unlock the text and change the height dimension to 2".

10.   Change the width dimension to 22".

11.   Select the uppercase letters, and from the top menu, click on the little down arrow beneath the 'Advanced' menu option.

12.   Choose 'Ungroup to letters.'

13.   You will notice that all the letters now have their own cut layer on the right-hand side.

14.   Starting from A, choose all the second letters of the alphabet and move them into the large grey square.

15.   Once they have all been moved, select them, and change the color to red.

16.   Select the remaining letters and change the color to gold.

17.   You can do the same for lowercase letters if you wish. For the sake of this project, there will only be the uppercase letters.

18.   Move and delete the large grey square.

19.   Save the project.

20.   Click 'Make it.'

21.   Design Space automatically puts the text onto two separate cutting sheets.

22.   Select cut number 1 and position the text into 2 or more rows to ensure they are well spaced out.

23.   Do the same for the second cut sheet.

24.   When you have the letters correctly lined up for cutting, press 'Continue.'

25.   Place the wooden board onto the purple cutting mat.

26.   Take the red vinyl and cut it to the size of the wood.

27.   Pull off the back of the vinyl sheet.

28.   Place transfer tape over the vinyl sheet, smoothing it down with the scraping tool.

29.   Apply the vinyl to the Cricut chipboard square and use the brayer or scraping tool to ensure it transfers correctly onto the chipboard.

30.   Slowly pull the transfer tape from the back of the vinyl.

31.   Carefully cover the corners of the wooden block with builder's tape to ensure the wood sticks to the purple cutting mat.

32.   Change the Cricut blade to the knife blade.

33.   Change the Cricut dial to the custom setting.

34.   Move the star wheels to the right-hand side of the feeding bar.

35.   Load the cutting sheet into the Cricut.

36.   In Design Space, choose the correct materials and press 'Continue.'

37.   When the Cricut is ready to cut, press 'Go.'

38.   It will take a bit of time to cut the wooden cutouts.

39.   When it is done with the first one, repeat the steps from 25 to 36 but use the green vinyl.

40.   While the Cricut is cutting out the second wood sheet of letters, remove the letters from the excess clipboard and clean them up using the weeder, knife, and tweezers.

41.   Glue the magnets onto the backs of each letter. Use 2 per letter, placing them strategically onto the wood.

42.   When they are done, they will make a lovely gift.

Chapter 17

Sugar Skull Wreath

R ecently, I grew an interest in sugar skulls. They are fun colors and exquisite Halloween designs. I shop on a weekly basis, and I was inspired by this during my last shopping. This is perfect for Halloween, and it gives that dangerous but sweet touch.

SUPPLIES NEEDED

- Foam Wreath

- Small spatula

- Marker

- Pencil

- Sanding block or sandpaper

- You would also need White acrylic paint

- Some black acrylic paint too

- Small detail paintbrush as well

- Felt flowers

- Toothpicks

STEP 1

Start by getting your design. Which you can make yourself, or you can download the template online. Then get your foam disc ready.

STEP 2

You make use of your black marker to trace out the shape of the template on your foam disk. And remember to keep the template disk because you would need it later.

STEP 3

You would make use of the foam cutter to cut out the shape of the sugar skull. You can make use of a Xacto knife if you do not have a foam cutter. After that, you are to make the surface of the foam smooth by making use of the small spatula. Doing this would add that smooth topcoat that you need and would also create a plaster-like sensation for your foam. For this project, I made use of the smooth finish for the first coat. Allowed it to dry then applied the second coat. When applying it, the layers should be as equal as possible and very smooth too. The front and the side should be covered completely. The back is not compulsory.

STEP 4

After both coats are smooth and dry, you should make use of your sanding block to smoothen the bumps that would affect that texture. You should make it gentle. Do not go too hard the smooth finishes sands easily. After that, you would take your white acrylic paint and give it one more last coat to prepare it for the sugar skull design and allow it to dry.

STEP 5

Get your template once more. This time you should make use of a pencil and trace over the design completely. You should make sure that you paint the solid potions. That you would be using for this transfer.

STEP 6

Turn your design over and place it on the form of the skull. Make sure that the side you painted with the pencil faces down. Next, you use your pencil to trace the complete design onto the foam. This should be very easy through the paper. You should be sure that you do not press it too hard. If not, you would imprint the foam with your pencil. It should look very much like the picture below.

STEP 7

With that small detail paint brush of yours, you should coat them with black acrylic paint to fill in your design. You may not choose to use the black and white design so you can paint your sugar skull whatever colors you like. You can also paint the outlines black to add more details, which gives it so much beauty.

STEP 8

Next, you can wrap your wreath with your black and white straps. That is what I did here. And for the flowers, you have been taught how to make felt flowers, apply that knowledge now. The leaves are basic leaf shape which you can just cut from some edges. Then you would pin all the felt flowers to that strategic side of the wreath. IF you do not want to use pins you can make use of hot glue a well as toothpicks to attach it.

If you are making use of toothpicks, you can put some behind the felt flowers then you carefully slide the foam skull to the point of the toothpick

STEP 9

This is the last step. You can get a stripped felt hanger for the wreath. This also adds that aesthetic value to the project or you simply leave it like that.

Chapter 18

Penguin Paper Bomb

I named this project penguin paper bomb! Because it is a bomb actually. Why? You can actually make the penguin bomb. This means that when you drop it, it will pop up. But that is a challenge for you. This project is a unique and a wonderful toy for your kids.

SUPPLIES NEEDED

- 65lb. 8.5" by 11" cardstock. This should be shared according to the color you want. I made use of two sheets of black, one sheet of white as well as another sheet of orange.

- Rubber bands. A particular one should be in size 16 which is 2.5 inches long while the other should be in size 18- 3 inches long

- Your Tacky glue is also needed

- Hot glue

- Two dimes or tinny weights.

- 7" piece of wire, tweezers or even a hooked took like a crochet hook or something else.

- Your Cricut machine for cutting

- Patterns or cut SVG files from free resource library or your own designs.

STEP 1

First, you upload the SVG file on your design space. You click on the Ungroup button then change the two red layers having the score lines to score, next you would choose the red score layer plus its following black cut layer then click Attach. There is a need for you to join both sides of the red scored layers and the black cut layers also. This would allow the score lines to appear in the right places.

STEP 2

You start first by folding the top of the headpiece. This is the smaller round piece that does not have a hole in the middle. Then you would fold the other side from the tab inwards. You should not forget to crease each tab to get that good fold. There is also a need for you to fold in the triangle pieces also. Then you would fold the rubber band tabs in then up. Below is a picture of the folded piece.

STEP 2

Next, you would glue down those triangles. Those rectangular side reinforcements should be on top each side having the triangles and the rubber band holders too. The photo below explains it all.

You should also do the same thing to the bottom of that headpiece. You fold and glue.

STEP 3

Next, you would fold the paper spring mechanism, which is divided into two major parts. The first part looks so much like a rectangle having wing; this part would be folded and glued to the base. That part, which is longer would go down again, just like it is in the picture.

STEP 4

Next, you would add your glue on the white-faced parts to the top and the bottom of the head piece like the picture below. You should pay so much attention to the orientation of those rubber band holders as you join the face parts to make sure they are in the right places altogether.

STEP 5

Next, you would join these two head pieces together with glue but make sure you fold the orange bill piece in half before you glue it then close it. Next, you would sandwich it between the top and the bottom of the white face, making use of the glue.

After the two head pieces are connected at the face, you would fold it close then glue all the other tabs and the rubber band holders together like the way it is in the picture below:

The head piece would have gotten its shape by this time.

STEP 6

Let us make the pop ability now. Just add a smaller rubber band which should be around size 16 to about 2.5" long then it would be folded and then drop it into the head so that one end of the rubber band would loop around on the end of the other rubber band loop.

Next, you would reach into the head, gasp the rubber band then you would hook it around the other end of that rubber band holding.

You may be having difficulties holding the rubber band. Just get a hook out of a small piece of wire like I did here.

Make use of this hook to reach into the head, especially from the opposite side of where the rubber band is placed. Hold onto the end of the rubber band and carefully hook it around the rubber band holding from the first one. This can be tricky.

Next, you would reach for the inside with the hook you have been able to make from the other part. Then you will get the rubber band and wrap it around the last end of the band holders.

It is at this moment you would able to let go of the head, and it would pop out into place immediately. Something like below:

STEP 7

You flatten the head one more time and turn it over. You should be sure that the mechanism is sticking out. There might be a need for you to reach in and pull it out. Then you would allow the protruding side of the mechanism to capture that part of the bottom; this would always keep it flat. Now drop it, it is time to work on the surface mechanism on the other side down. Check to be sure that there is nothing impeding the mechanism from being pushed, especially when it lands on that work surface.

Next, you would fold the two halves on that penguin's body.

Glue down the triangles, as well as the side reinforcements pieces as well as rubber band holders. The same way you did for the head pieces.

Attach the glue on the white body pieces. You should watch closely, the arrangement of the black body pieces. You can do the same orientation just like the photos

Now insert that hook and size 18 rubber band into the body in the same way you did for the head.

This is the body with the rubber band in one place

Next, you would use the glue to attach to the head of the body. Then line up the rectangles on each side so that they would match up. Then you would glue it. If the body is not aligning to the right, you can turn it over and then try it once again. When you glue it, you should center that head on the body as straight as possible.

STEP 8

You would glue the reinforcement piece onto the base of the penguin paper bomb you should be careful not to impede the mechanism present in the middle. Check the picture below to see if it fits properly.

Then you would paste the orange feet so that they would stick out on both sides of the white part of the body.

Next, you would stand your penguin up, and you would paste the wings on both sides of its body. You should make use of strong glue so that the wings would not brush the ground. Furthermore, this would help the penguin when it jumps.

Another way you to increase stability is by placing two dimes glued onto the bottom. This would help it stabilize its weight when it pops up.

This time, you will try it out if your penguin paper bomb is really a bomb. You flatten him then you would place that mechanism in place then drop it onto that surface. Did its pop you? be sure that there is nothing coming in the way of the tab. Free it, if you find something stopping it so that it does not impede the mechanism.

Chapter 19

Personalized Baby Clothing and

Peace Sign Tank Top

Materials needed – "Cricut Maker" or "Cricut Explore", standard grip mat, "Cricut" iron-on or heat transfer vinyl, "Cricut Easy Press", "Easy Press" mat, weeding tool, baby body suit.

Step 1

Log into the "Design Space" application and click on the "New Project" button on the top right corner of the screen to view a blank canvas.

Step 2

Click on the "Images" icon on the "Design Panel" and type in "pink journey" in the search bar to narrow your search for the images used in the project. Select any other image that may caught your eye and click on "Insert Images" at the bottom of the screen.

Step 3

Your selected images will appear stacked up on the Canvas, as shown in the picture below. Now, click on the "Text" icon and type in "I KNOW… (press enter twice) I AM BEAUTIFUL!!!".

Step 4

For the image below, the font "Anna's Fancy Lettering – Hannah" in Regular as shown in the picture below was selected. Edit the image as needed and group the images together by clicking on the "Group" icon.

Step 5

Save the project and your design is ready to be printed and cut. Simply click on the "Make It" button. Place the iron-on with the shiny side down on the cutting mat then load it to your "Cricut" machine and follow the instructions on the screen to cut your project. (Make sure to mirror the image).

Step 6

Carefully remove the excess material from the sheet using the "weeder tool", making sure only the design remains on the clear liner.

Step 7

Using the "Cricut Easy Press" and "Easy Press Mat" the iron-on layers can be easily transferred to your sock. The recommended temperature for everyday iron-on material and cotton base material is 330 °F. So preheat your "Easy Press".

Step 8

Put your design on the desired area and apply pressure for 30 seconds. Then flip your sock to apply the heat and pressure for another 15 seconds on the other side.

Peace Sign Tank Top

Materials needed – "Cricut Maker" or "Cricut Explore", standard grip mat (12 x 24 inches), Cricut foil iron-on in rose gold, black tank top, "Cricut Easy Press", "Easy Press" mat, weeder.

Step 1

Log into the "Design Space" application and click on the "New Project" button on the top right corner of the screen to view a blank canvas.

Step 2

Click on the "Projects" icon and type in "peace sign shirt" in the search bar.

Step 3

Click on "Customize" to further edit the project to your preference or simply click on the "Make It" button. Place the iron-on with the shiny side down on the cutting mat then load it to your "Cricut" machine and follow the instructions on the screen to cut your project. (Make sure to mirror the image).

Step 5

Carefully remove the excess material from the sheet using the "weeder tool", making sure only the design remains on the clear liner.

Step 6

Using the "Cricut Easy Press" and "Easy Press Mat" the iron-on layers can be easily transferred to your tank top. The recommended temperature for everyday iron-on material and cotton base material is 330 °F. So preheat your "Easy Press".

Step 7

Use the "Easy Press" to get rid of any wrinkles from your transfer target area by pressing on it for 5 seconds. Then put your design on the area and heat the area while applying pressure for 30 seconds and flip your tank top to apply the heat and pressure for another 15 seconds. (Note – If your design is larger than the size of your "Easy Press", then apply pressure for 30 seconds on each side of the design and a little bit of overlap would not cause any damage to the design).

Chapter 20

Sassy Leather Jacket and Southwest Lizard Shoes

Materials needed – "Cricut Maker" or "Cricut Explore", standard grip mat (12 x 24 inches), Cricut foil iron-on in rose gold, baby leather jacket, "Cricut Easy Press", "Easy Press" mat, weeder.

Step 1

Log into the "Design Space" application and click on the "New Project" button on the top right corner of the screen to view a blank canvas.

Step 2

Click on the "Images" icon on the "Design Panel" and type in "#M3F5747" in the search bar. Select the image and click on the "Insert Images" button at the bottom of the screen.

Step 3

Edit the project to your preference or simply click on the "Make It" button. Place the iron-on with the shiny side down on the cutting mat then load it to your "Cricut" machine and follow the instructions on the screen to cut your project. (Make sure to mirror the image).

Step 5

Carefully remove the excess material from the sheet using the "weeder tool", making sure only the design remains on the clear liner.

Step 6

Using the "Cricut Easy Press" and "Easy Press Mat" the iron-on layers can be easily transferred to your jacket. The recommended temperature for everyday iron-on material and cotton base material is 330 °F. So preheat your "Easy Press".

Step 7

Use the "Easy Press" to get rid of any wrinkles from your transfer target area by pressing on it for 5 seconds. Then put your design on the area and heat the area while applying pressure for 30 seconds and flip your jacket to apply the heat and pressure for another 15 seconds. (Note – If your design is larger than the size of your "Easy Press", then apply pressure for 30 seconds on each side of the design and a little bit of overlap would not cause any damage to the design).

Southwest Lizard Shoes

Materials needed – "Cricut Maker" or "Cricut Explore", standard grip mat, Cricut iron-on lite, high top sneakers, "Cricut Easy Press", press cloth, weeder.

Step 1

Log into the "Design Space" application and click on the "New Project" button on the top right corner of the screen to view a blank canvas.

Step 2

Click on the "Projects" icon and type in "lizard shoes" in the search bar.

Step 3

Click on "Customize" to further edit the project to your preference or simply click on the "Make It" button. Place the iron-on with the shiny side down on the cutting mat then load it to your "Cricut" machine and follow the instructions on the screen to cut your project. (Make sure to mirror the image).

Step 5

Carefully remove the excess material from the sheet using the "weeder tool", making sure only the design remains on the clear liner.

Step 6

Using the "Cricut Easy Press" and "Easy Press Mat" the iron-on layers can be easily transferred to your tank top. The recommended temperature for everyday iron-on material and cotton base material is 330 °F. So preheat your "Easy Press".

Step 7

Use the "Easy Press" to get rid of any wrinkles from your transfer target area by pressing on it for 5 seconds. Then put your design on the area and heat the area while applying pressure for 30 seconds and repeat the same on the other shoe.

Chapter 21

Thanksgiving Table Runner and

Pinecone Turkey

Project thanks to Cricut Design Space

D ress up your table with a festive table runner, tablecloth, or place mat with a quick and easy iron-on decal. Add shapes, images, or phrases to fit any occasion. To complete this project; all you need is a tablecloth or runner, gold iron-on vinyl, and an iron.

Step 1

Open Design Space and write out any text you want to appear on your runner. Add any images from your design library and place them around your text as preferred.

Step 2

Cut out your iron-on image and use the weeding tool for any additional pieces that are not meant to be part of the design.

Step 3

Place your design vinyl-side down on your runner in the center or the location you prefer. Turn on your iron to the "cotton" setting and place on top of the paper backing of your design and let it set for about 15 seconds. Continue moving your iron around to adhere your design to the runner.

Step 4

Remove the paper backing when your image is transferred and decorate the table with your new design!

Pinecone Turkey

Project thanks to 100 Directions

Another fun holiday project is a craft where you can have children help you. You can decorate their place settings at a holiday meal. You

219

will need to gather a few pinecones in good condition, a variety of cardstock in Thanksgiving colors (orange, green, yellow, brown, etc.) or just in white, glue, and any additional embellishments you want.

Step 1

In Design Space, Create the turkey head shape and the feather shapes. You can create one feather template or several different options. Large turkeys can have about five feathers and smaller have about four. You can also vary the feather shapes per turkey.

Step 2

Print your images. Print them separately on colored paper or design your images with color and print them on white paper so the colors show up vibrantly.

Step 3

Cut out the turkey heads and feathers. Add any embellishments to the feathers or heads, like gluing on real feathers or twine. You can also pinch the ends of the feathers to make them more dimensional.

Step 4

Add a drop of glue to the end of the feathers and the neck of the turkey head and place them into the pinecones. Allow the glue to dry fully.

Chapter 22

Pie Stencil and Leftover Boxes

Project thanks to Cricut Design Space

nother holiday project can come in the form of a sweet treat using this stencil for the powdered sugar. If you want a smaller idea, adapt this same concept to fit the inside of a coffee mug. Sprinkle cinnamon or another spice over the top of your latte for a lovely morning pick-me-up.

For this project you need cardstock and a weeding tool, in addition to your pie and powdered sugar.

Step 1

Write your message in Design Space. Make sure to adjust your font size and layout to fit the dimensions of your pie.

Step 2

Cut out your words from the cardstock and weed out the center of any letters you do not want to be part of the design.

Step 3

Place the cardstock over your pie. Consider placing a piece of wax paper around the edges of your pie to rest the stencils on so the paper does not rest on the pie directly.

Step 4

Using a sister, sift the powdered sugar over the top of the stencil. When finished, gently and carefully lift the stencil off the pie to reveal the message. Remove the wax paper and throw away. Serve the pie as soon as possible after using the sugar to minimize any changes to the sugary message.

Leftover Boxes

Project thanks to Designer Trapped

Send your guests off in style with these adorable leftover boxes. This two-step project combines customized stickers and sweet little boxes. If you want to, skip the boxes, and attach the stickers to store bought bags or other containers. Or go wild and offer guests a combination of to-go containers to choose from!

Pick up a few pages of sticker paper and cardstock that is corrugated cardboard. Look for interesting patterns or keep it simple if you prefer. The cardboard will be used for the bottom of your to-go boxes. Purchase coordinating traditional cardstock to make the lid to the boxes. Additionally, you will need glue or glue tape to adhere the edges of the box together. If you are offering guests a variety of to-go options, like bags or other, store-bought boxes, make sure to pick some of those up as well for your stickers.

Step 1

Design your sticker template. Include a nice border from the Design Space Library, and text indicating when the leftovers were from to help guests keep track of how long they have had the leftovers. Adjust the size of your stickers to fit the to-go boxes, about 1.75" X 1.5", and to attach to other bags or boxes, about 5' X 4".

Step 2

Print your stickers and then cut them apart using your Cricut.

Step 3

In Design Space Library, search for the pie box template. It is free and easy to load! Print and cut your boxes; load the cardboard for the bottom of the boxes and the traditional cardstock for the top.

Step 4

Part of the cut file from Design Space is instruction for the machine to score your boxes to make assembly easier. Fold along the scored lines and use your glue to attach the edges together. Assemble the tops and bottoms with the same method.

Step 5

Add a sticker to the top of your boxes. If you are using other containers or bags, attach your stickers to them as well.

Chapter 23

Photo Envelope Liners and Geo Bowl

Project thanks to Glamour and Grace

I f you are preparing letters for a special occasion, dress up the envelop with something special. Add a photo of your big event to you thank you card envelopes, or a funny image to a birthday card envelope.

Customize the inside of your envelopes to show your loved ones that you are thinking about them, even before they have a chance to read the words you wrote.

For the best results, print your images on photo paper, especially if you are using photographs. Your project will fit 5X7 envelopes, so pick up several that are the paper and color you want. Finally, to attach the photos professionally on the inside of the envelopes, make sure you have a roll or two of double-sided tape.

Step 1

Choose the photograph that you want to put inside the envelopes. You can choose one or can choose a variety of images. Make sure the images are appropriate for cropping the top edges to fit the envelope flap. In addition, your image needs to be at least seven inches wide to fit the 5X7 envelope.

Step 2

In Design Space, upload the envelope liner template. Select "simple image," and do not feel required to delete a backdrop. Move to the next screen and select "save as a Cut Image."

Step 3

In the workspace, insert your image and pull the corners until it fits the envelope size, in this case seven inches. To help the envelope fold better along the flap, insert a score line on your image so that it sits along the fold line.

Step 4

Print your image on photo paper and then loan on your cutting matt to trim and score.

Step 5

Take your photo off your cutting matt and fold it along the score line. Use your scraper tool to get a good fold line.

Step 6

Slide your image into your envelope and attach with the double-sided tape. Make sure to add enough tape to securely fasten the image to the envelope.

Step 7

Use your scraper to press the image into the envelope and smooth it over to make sure it is firmly attached.

Step 8

Insert your card or message, seal and send! You are sure to get a few appreciative comments soon.

Geo Bowl

Project thanks to Vintage Revivals

This intricate-looking project is a breeze to construct. Add a pop of modern glam to your décor or fill it with special treats and give it as a gift. You can use a combination of colors, but the white exterior with the golden metallic center adds to its modern aesthetic. For this project, pick up two pieces of cardstock in the colors you determine, heat up your hot glue gun, and get ready for a simple and amazing project.

Step 1

Open Design Space and look for the design under "Make It Now." It is labeled "Geo Ball."

Step 2

Load your paper onto your mat and create your designs. Make sure you are set up to score your paper and not cut it!

Step 3

After your project is done, remove it from your mat and place your pieces together, gluing them to make sure they stick together.

Step 4

Fold your project so the white paper is on the outside and glue it together along the edges. For additional tips, read the instructions from the "Make It Now" file.

Chapter 24

Model Airplane and Art Journals

O ne of the newest accessories Cricut has released is the Cricut Knife Blade. This amazing new tool can complete even more projects, making your Cricut more useful than ever. Two types of wood that are best for this project and the new tool include Basswood and Balsa wood. This material is a little thicker but still pliable. They have been used in model building for a long time. Balsa wood tends to be cheaper, thinner, and easier to find than Basswood.

This project is preloaded in Cricut Design Space under "Make It Now." You will want to get two pieces of Balsa wood, both about 1/32 inch thick. Stain one piece a darker color and leave the other piece its natural color (off white). To add a custom name to your project, you will want a piece of vinyl in a coordinating color. You will also want wood glue or super glue to secure the pieces in place after you construct it. Consider making the project for decoration or giving the pieces as a kit for a present.

Step 1

Begin in Design Space and open the "Make It Now" file for the model airplane. Load your balsa wood onto a Strong Grip Adhesive mat. Adjust your settings to "Custom." When you are ready, press "Go."

Step 2

Once your project has cut once, leave your wood on the mat, and go over it again three or four more times to make sure it is cut through.

Step 3

Remove your wood from your cutting mat, being careful not to break any pieces while you remove it. Put them aside for a moment.

Step 4

In Design Space, write out the name or create the details you want to appear on your airplane. Load your vinyl on your cutting mat and press "Go."

Step 5

Once your vinyl has printed, weed out any parts of your design you do not want. Transfer the vinyl to your airplane piece.

Step 6

If you are assembling your airplane, use your glue to make sure all the pieces are firmly attached together. Display in a prominent place on a shelf or suspended by fishing line from the ceiling.

Art Journals

These sweet little notebooks are great for art and travel journals, but you can really customize them to fit any need or desire. Choose favorite colors and patterns, personalized sayings, or words, and you can even add a few more pages to the inside if you want. Get ready for some serious jealous looks the next time you pull one of these out of your bag!

You will need:

Glue

Colored thread

Large needle

Paper piercer or something to poke holes in your paper

Various cardstock in interesting prints

Various paper in interesting colors and prints

Step 1

In Design Space, create a square on your canvas. Round the corners. You may want to ungroup the layers and delete the bottom layer. Also, adjust the size of your square to the size of your final notebook. For example, in this example, the notebooks are 5" x 7". This means your square will need to measure 10" x 7".

Step 2

Add your score line to the middle of the square or rectangle shape. You will find this line under "lines." Adjust the size to fit your project and then select "Align" and "Center." This should automatically adjust the line, so it is directly in the middle of your project.

Step 3

Next, add notches to your center score line to tell you where to pierce your paper. You can place another score line at 90 degrees from the centerline and scale it down, so it is small. Alternatively, you can place a very small circle over the place you want to pierce your paper and have the machine cut the little spot out for you. Measure down about one inch from the top and bottom to place your holes or notches.

Step 4

If you want to add any custom cut outs or stickers to the front cover, you can now design those as you desire. Otherwise, you can use shapes and stickers you already have on hand. You can always create these later as well.

Step 5

Now you are ready to create the inside pages of your book. You will want to copy and paste the cover rectangle piece and make the pages just slightly smaller than the cover. Consider the size 9.8" x 6.8". This means you will also want to re-align your center score line. You will also need to adjust the size. Do not move your notch or hole marks, though! Keep that one inch from the top and bottom of the cover, not the page!

Step 6

If you moved the notches or hole marks, you could always group the markings from the cover and copy and paste them for as many pages of the book you are creating. Then move, do not resize, these markings and place them over the centerline of each page.

Step 7

If you want to add images and cut outs to the internal pages, you can add those now. Keep in mind that any words you cut out on one side of the page will appear back on the other side! Consider using images and shapes to be safe. You can also create vinyl stickers or drawn images to the pages if you do not want to cut into the paper. If you choose vinyl words or images, some art mediums may struggle to cover them properly.

Step 8

When you are done designing your pages, send your file to print, cut, and score your cover and pages. Follow the prompts to load your paper and tools into your machine.

Step 9

After your pages and cover are cut, fold on the score line, and place the pages into the cover and line up the notches or holes. If you are using notches, use your paper punch to poke holes in the cover and paper where the notches are located. Depending on your paper, you may want to punch holes one at a time.

Step 10

Thread your needle with the colored thread. Pass your needle through the holes and tie a slip knot. Tighten your knot as tight as possible and then tie off with a regular knot. You can tie on the outside of the journal or on the inside. Trim the threads as short as you want.

Step 11

If you are decorating your cover, make sure you add stickers or vinyl to the cover as you prefer. Now you are ready to start journaling away!

Chapter 25

Paper Succulents in a Container and Giant Paper Flowers

This pretty little project can be made to fit into any container you already have and can instantly add a little punch to your mantelpiece, table setting, or display. Make as many or as few of these different succulents as you want.

You will need:

Cardstock in teals and pinks

Ink pads in different coordinating colors of teal and pink

Sponges or dabbers for the ink

Hot glue gun

Foam to fill your container

Step 1

In Design Space, look for the design file for succulents. If you want to create the design yourself, create one large petal shaped flower and then copy it about six times. Scale each copy down to a smaller size. If you need to, remove a petal or two to make it appear more proportional. For the spiral and pointed succulent, make a spiral with three rings. The center of the ring should be a circle on the end. Add pointed triangles to the outside of the spiral lines.

Step 2

Once you have your designs ready, send your file to cut on your different colored card stock. Remove your pieces and place corresponding flower pieces together on a covered work surface. Using your sponges or dabbers, add a touch of ink to the outer edges of each petal shape or on the tips of the spikes of the spiral. You can keep the colors matching or contrast with a pink tip on a teal succulent and vice versa.

Step 3

Gently curl the edges of the petals up on the ends to make them more three-dimensional.

Step 4

Using your hot glue gun, glue the layers of the succulents together and roll the pointed succulents and glue them together as well.

Step 5

Place the floral foam inside your container, about ½ inch from the top. You can place your succulents on the foam or glue them down in the place where you like the arrangement. Once all your succulents are placed, consider covering the exposed foam with paper grass or shredded paper. You can glue this covering down if you like but it typically looks best when it is loose.

Giant Paper Flowers

Glam up a nursery wall, a hallway, a party, wedding, or any other notable event or space with these amazing flowers! Get creative with the colors or even try out patterned paper for a totally different effect.

You will need:

A marker for rolling petals

Hot glue gun

Pink cardstock, at least 17 pages

Flower file from Design Space library

Step 1

Open the flower file in Design Space. It will make a 3-inch circular base, 2 petals for the interior rosebud, 6 4-inch smaller petals, 8 5.5-inch medium petals, 8 7-inch large petals, and 8 8-inch extra-large petals. The file will appear that all the petals are overlapping—it is ok and will cut properly once you hit "Make It." Be prepared to send your file to cut and use all 17 sheets of paper. If you are not using a file from the Cricut library, use the dimensions described above to make your own petal shapes.

Step 2

Once all the petals are cut out, glue the bottoms of the petals together with your hot glue gun so it creates a cupped shape to the petal. It is best to do a single line of glue on one side of the slit in the petal base and then overlaps the other side and press gently. This is for all the extra-large, large, medium, and small petals.

Step 3

To shape the outer edge of each petal, use the marker and roll the petal outwards. You can curl only the top of the petals, but you can also experiment with rolling the sides as well. In addition, make sure to roll the petals out, not in. It will look better when finished.

Step 4

Create the interior rosebud now. Apply glue to one edge of a petal and roll it inside and attach it to another petal. Roll that petal and glue it to the edge of the first petal. Leave about ½-inch in the center, about the size of your pointer finger. Take the other petals and wrap them around the first, gluing them in place, but with about another ½-inch in between the petals.

Step 5

Add the small petals to the rosebud. Glue them around the rosebud trying to keep that ½-inch distance between each petal for best results. Set the rosebud aside for now.

Step 6

Take your base and your extra-large petals and begin gluing the petals to the base. Dab a few spots of glue on the bottom, the underside of the petals and press them to the outer edge of the base. Start with one petal on one side and then the next petal on the opposite side of the base. Use two more petals to fill in the spaces between the two. Create another layer of extra-large petals, adjusting the petals so they overlap, not sit evenly on one another. Then move to the large petals, creating two layers again. Repeat the same for the medium layers. Use four small pieces to create one layer of small petals on the inside of the flower base.

Step 7

Take the remaining two small petals and glue them around your rosebud. If you want, for aesthetics, use your marker to roll the smaller petals inwards towards the rosebud.

Step 8

Apply hot glue generously to the bottom of the rosebud and press it firmly into the center of your flower base. Adjust your petal curves with your marker if you need to, but you should be ready to decorate!

Conclusion

Beauty is a thing of joy forever; someone has said this. Nature itself is very beautiful. Using artificial tools and things to create something beautiful with just one natural idea is a quality of human. Humanmade thing and natural thing, your surrounding is abundant with it. Creativity comes from the soul, artists are not born only sometimes artistic things come to you by practicing more and more. Translating your soul into creativity in dimension of using vinyl craft gives you very fabulous items or products. Human always wants variety of things around his surroundings. Creative arts fascinate them and motivate them. Getting bore from boring things are common but creativity freshens you up.

Innovation along technology and science gives you a finest product. Field of art and crafts is encouraged; their importance is understandable in today's world. Vinyl craft is adding another new chapter in the world of art and craft. The material used in vinyl art is very cheaper and easily available in the market. Only you need to gain a little knowledge about vinyl crafting, get bit experience with its use and you are ready to make something very creative and useable item. Use and implication of vinyl art is very wide. Rest is all about your idea your way of judging the beauty and looking perception. This book is a little effort to facilitate you with some innovative ideas. Add more ideas to these mentioned ideas and get an item in more innovative way.

If you have worked your way through the projects in this book, you are well on your way to becoming a Cricut pro. Like a recipe book, the projects, along with the ideas in this book, can be adjusted, adapted, and added to so that you can make each one uniquely yours.

With the Cricut, you are going to find birthdays, special occasions, seasonal holidays, and even school projects are a lot easier as well as more personalized. Everyone loves receiving gifts, cards, and so on that have been designed especially for them.

You do not have to stop at just making gifts for family and friends; you can even sell your specially designed crafts at markets or online. My book "Cricut for Beginners" has loads of ideas on where and how to sell your crafts. It also has handy tips, advice, and a few more design ideas on the Cricut, the materials, and so on.

Happy Circuiting and keep crafty!

CPSIA information can be obtained
at www.ICGtesting.com
Printed in the USA
LVHW070126071220
673511LV00051B/2236

9 781801 093019